MY LITTLE
CHOCOLATE BOOK

MORE THAN 80
IRRESISTIBLE RECIPES

MURDOCH BOOKS

CONTENTS

LITTLE CAKES,
COOKIES
AND SLICES

WHITE CHOCOLATE AND ALMOND CAKES

PREPARATION 30 MINUTES
COOKING 30 MINUTES
MAKES 12

140 g (5 oz/1 cup) chopped white chocolate
85 g (3 oz) chopped unsalted butter
125 ml (4 fl oz/½ cup) milk
115 g (4 oz/½ cup) caster (superfine) sugar
1 egg, at room temperature
115 g (4 oz/¾ cup) self-raising flour, sifted
55 g (2 oz/½ cup) ground almonds
12 raspberries and icing (confectioners') sugar, to serve

WHITE CHOCOLATE GANACHE
400 g (15½ oz) finely chopped white chocolate
170 ml (5½ fl oz/⅔ cup) cream

METHOD
Preheat the oven to 190°C (375°F/Gas 5). Line a
12-hole muffin tray with paper cases.

Combine the chocolate, butter and milk in a saucepan.
Stir over low heat until melted and smooth. Transfer
to a bowl and set aside to cool a little. Whisk in the
sugar and egg.

Combine the flour and ground almonds, then add
to the bowl and mix well. Spoon into the muffin holes
and bake for 20 minutes, or until a skewer comes
out clean when poked into the centre of a cake.
Leave in the tray for 5 minutes before transferring
to a wire rack to cool.

Meanwhile, to make the white chocolate ganache,
place the chocolate in a heatproof bowl. Heat the
cream in a saucepan until it is almost simmering. Add
to the chocolate and leave for 1 minute, then stir until
smooth. Cool in the fridge, stirring occasionally, until
the ganache has a thick, spreadable consistency.

To serve, spread the ganache over the cakes. Top each
one with a raspberry and dust with a little icing sugar.

BUTTERFLY CHOCOLATE CAKES

PREPARATION 20 MINUTES
COOKING 20 MINUTES
MAKES 24

60 g (2¼ oz) unsalted butter, softened
80 g (2¾ oz/⅓ cup firmly packed) soft brown sugar
½ teaspoon vanilla extract
1 egg, at room temperature
60 g (2½ oz/¼ cup) self-raising flour
30 g (1 oz/¼ cup) unsweetened cocoa powder
2 tablespoons milk
60 g (2 oz/¼ cup) thick (double/heavy) cream
80 g (2¾ oz/¼ cup) raspberry jam
icing (confectioners') sugar, to dust

METHOD
Preheat the oven to 180°C (350°F/Gas 4). Line two
12-hole muffin trays with paper cases.

Beat the butter, sugar and vanilla until pale and creamy. Add the egg and beat well. Sift together the flour and cocoa. Add half the flour mixture to the butter and whisk gently, then add the milk and combine. Add the rest of the flour and mix well.

Divide evenly among the paper cases. Bake for 15–20 minutes, or until a skewer comes out clean when poked into the centre of a cake. Transfer to a wire rack to cool.

Cut a shallow round from the centre of each cake, then cut the round in half. Fill the centres of the cakes with a little cream and some raspberry jam. Position the two cake wedges on the cream, pressing them down very gently to resemble butterfly wings. Dust with sifted icing sugar.

CHOCOLATE MUFFINS

PREPARATION 15 MINUTES
COOKING 25 MINUTES
MAKES 12

310 g (11 oz/2½ cups) self-raising flour
40 g (1½ oz/⅓ cup) unsweetened cocoa powder
½ teaspoon bicarbonate of soda (baking soda)
145 g (5 oz/⅔ cup) caster (superfine) sugar
375 ml (13 fl oz/1½ cups) buttermilk
2 eggs, at room temperature
160 g (5½ oz) unsalted butter, melted and cooled

METHOD
Preheat the oven to 200°C (400°F/Gas 6). Lightly
grease a 12-hole muffin tray. Sift the flour, cocoa
powder and bicarbonate of soda into a bowl and
add the sugar. Make a well in the centre.

In a jug, whisk together the buttermilk and eggs
and pour into the well. Gently fold in the butter
with a metal spoon. Do not overmix — the mixture
should still be lumpy.

Fill each hole about three-quarters full. Bake for
20–25 minutes, or until a skewer comes out clean
when poked into the centre of a muffin. Leave the
muffins in the tray for 5 minutes. Transfer to a wire
rack to cool. Serve warm or at room temperature.

CHOCOLATE BEETROOT CAKES

PREPARATION 20 MINUTES
COOKING 20 MINUTES
MAKES 8

cooking oil spray
125 g (4½ oz/1 cup) plain (all-purpose) flour
40 g (11½ oz/⅓ cup) unsweetened cocoa powder
1½ teaspoons bicarbonate of soda (baking soda)
½ teaspoon baking powder
1 teaspoon mixed spice
230 g (8 oz/1 cup firmly packed) soft brown sugar
75 g (2½ oz/¾ cup) walnut halves, chopped
170 ml (5½ fl oz/⅔ cup) canola or vegetable oil
2 eggs, at room temperature
225 g (8 oz) beetroot, finely shredded

CHOCOLATE DRIZZLE ICING
195 g (6¾ oz/1¼ cups) icing (confectioners') sugar
30 g (1 oz/¼ cup) unsweetened cocoa powder

METHOD
Preheat the oven to 180°C (350°F/Gas 4).
Spray 8 ramekins with oil to grease and place on
a large baking tray.

Sift together the flour, cocoa, bicarbonate of soda,
baking powder and mixed spice. Stir in the sugar and
walnuts, then make a well in the centre.

Whisk together the vegetable oil and eggs. Add the
beetroot and stir. Pour into the well and, using a large
metal spoon, fold them together. Divide the mixture
among the ramekins and smooth the surfaces.

Bake for 20 minutes, or until a skewer comes out
clean when poked into the centre of a cake. Leave the
cakes in the ramekins for 5 minutes before turning
them out onto a wire rack to cool.

To make the chocolate drizzle icing, sift together
the icing sugar and cocoa. Add 60 ml (2 fl oz/¼ cup)
boiling water and mix until smooth. Drizzle the cakes
with the icing. Set aside for 30 minutes, or until the
icing is set. Serve with thick cream or ice cream.

CHEESECAKES WITH MIXED BERRIES

PREPARATION 20 MINUTES
COOKING 30 MINUTES
MAKES 4

4 butternut biscuits (cookies)
85 g (2 oz/½ cup) white chocolate chips
250 g (9 oz/1 cup) cream cheese, at room temperature
60 ml (2 fl oz/¼ cup) cream, for whipping
115 g (4 oz/½ cup) caster (superfine) sugar
1 egg, at room temperature
250 g (9 oz/1½–2 cups) mixed berries, such as
raspberries, blueberries and sliced strawberries
Framboise or Cointreau

METHOD
Preheat the oven to 160°C (315°F/Gas 2–3). Grease a
four-hole muffin tray and line each with two strips of
baking paper to make a cross pattern.

Put a biscuit in the base of each hole. Put the chocolate in a heatproof bowl. Half fill a saucepan with water, bring to the boil, then remove from the heat and sit the bowl over the pan (don't let the bowl touch the water or the chocolate will get too hot and seize). Stir occasionally, until the chocolate melts.

Using electric beaters, beat the cream cheese, cream and half the sugar until thick and smooth. Beat in the egg and then the melted chocolate. Pour evenly into the muffin holes and bake for 25 minutes, or until set. Cool completely in the tray, then carefully run a small spatula or flat-bladed knife around the edge and lift out of the holes using the paper strips as handles. Refrigerate for 1 hour, or until ready to serve.

Place the berries in a bowl and fold in the remaining sugar. Leave for 10–15 minutes, or until juices form. Flavour with a little liqueur. Serve the cheesecakes topped with the berries.

CHOCOLATE RAISIN SCROLLS

PREPARATION 20 MINUTES
COOKING 1 HOUR 25 MINUTES
MAKES 8

375 g (1 lb/3 cups) plain (all-purpose) flour, sifted
2 tablespoons caster (superfine) sugar
2 teaspoons dried yeast
finely grated zest of 1 lemon
185 ml (6 fl oz/¾ cup) lukewarm milk
125 g (4½ oz) unsalted butter, diced and softened
2 egg yolks, at room temperature, lightly whisked
icing (confectioners') sugar, to dust

FILLING
100 g (3½ oz/⅔ cup) chopped dark chocolate
90 g (3¼ oz/¾ cup) raisins
80 g (2¾ oz/¾ cup) chopped toasted pecans
55 g (2 oz/¼ cup) soft brown sugar
60 g (2¼ oz) unsalted butter, finely diced

METHOD
Combine the flour, sugar, yeast, ½ teaspoon salt and
lemon zest and make a well in the centre. Add the
milk, butter and egg yolks. Use a wooden spoon and
then your hands to mix a soft, but not sticky, dough.

Turn the dough onto a lightly floured surface and knead for 5 minutes or until smooth and elastic. Grease a bowl with unsalted butter. Shape the dough into a ball, place in the bowl and cover with plastic wrap. Place in a warm, draught-free place for 1½ hours or until doubled in size.

To make the filling, combine the chocolate, raisins, pecans, brown sugar and unsalted butter. Stir until evenly combined. Set aside.

Place eight 185 ml (6½ fl oz/¾ cup) straight-sided paper cups on a baking tray.

Use your fist to knock down the dough. Knead on a lightly floured surface for 2 minutes, or until returned to its original size. Use a lightly floured rolling pin to roll the dough to a 25 x 45 cm (10 x 18 inch) rectangle with a long side closest to you. Spread the filling evenly over the dough, leaving a 5 cm (2 inch) border along the top end. Starting with the long side closest to you, roll up the dough to enclose the filling. Cut the roll into eight even slices, each about 5 cm (2 inch) thick, and place, cut side up, in the paper cases. Brush the tops with milk and cover with plastic wrap. Place in a warm, draught-free place for 30 minutes or until well risen.

Preheat oven to 190°C (375°F/Gas 5). Brush the scrolls with a little milk and bake for 10 minutes. Reduce the oven to 180°C (350°F/Gas 4) and cook for a further 15 minutes, or until cooked through. Serve warm.

CHOCOLATE SAUCE

PREPARATION 5 MINUTES
COOKING 5 MINUTES
SERVES 8

250 g (9 oz/1⅔ cups) chopped dark chocolate
185 ml (6 fl oz/¾ cup) cream
50 g (1¾ oz) chopped unsalted butter

METHOD
To make the chocolate sauce, put the chocolate,
cream and butter in a saucepan. Stir over low heat
until the chocolate has melted and the mixture is
smooth. Drizzle over the cake or dessert of your
choice and serve.

CHOCOLATE CHIP COOKIES

PREPARATION 20 MINUTES
COOKING 15 MINUTES
MAKES 40

185 g (6½ oz/1½ cups) plain (all-purpose) flour
90 g (3¼ oz/¾ cup) unsweetened cocoa powder
280 g (10 oz/1½ cups) soft brown sugar
180 g (6½ oz) unsalted butter, cubed
150 g (5 oz/1 cup) chopped dark chocolate
3 eggs, at room temperature, lightly beaten
265 g (9¼ oz/1½ cups) chocolate bits

METHOD
Preheat the oven to 180°C (350°F/Gas 4). Line two
baking trays with baking paper. Sift the flour and
cocoa into a large bowl, add the sugar and make a
well in the centre.

Put butter and chocolate in a small heatproof bowl.
Bring a saucepan of water to the boil, then remove
from the heat. Sit the bowl over the saucepan. Stir
occasionally, until the chocolate and butter have
melted and are smooth. Combine the butter, chocolate
and eggs with the dry ingredients. Stir in the chocolate
bits. Drop tablespoons of the mixture onto the trays,
allow room for spreading. Bake for 7–10 minutes, or
until firm to touch. Cool on the trays for 5 minutes
before transferring to a wire rack to cool completely.

TOLLHOUSE COOKIES

PREPARATION 20 MINUTES
COOKING 10 MINUTES
MAKES 40

180 g (6½ oz) unsalted butter, cubed and softened
140 g (5 oz/¾ cup) soft brown sugar
110 g (3¾ oz/½ cup) sugar
2 eggs, at room temperature, lightly beaten
1 teaspoon vanilla extract
280 g (10 oz/2¼ cups) plain (all-purpose) flour
1 teaspoon bicarbonate of soda (baking soda)
350 g (12 oz/2 cups) dark chocolate bits
100 g (3½ oz/1 cup) pecans, roughly chopped

METHOD
Preheat the oven to 190°C (375°F/Gas 5). Line two
baking trays with baking paper.

Cream the butter and sugars with electric beaters until
light and fluffy. Gradually add the egg, beating well
after each addition. Stir in the vanilla, then the sifted
flour and bicarbonate of soda until just combined.
Mix in the chocolate bits and pecans. Drop
tablespoons of mixture onto the trays; leave room for
spreading. Bake the cookies for 8–10 minutes, or until
lightly golden. Cool on the trays before transferring to
a wire rack to cool completely. When completely cold,
store in an airtight container.

CHOCOLATE HAZELNUT SPIRALS

PREPARATION 20 MINUTES
COOKING 12 MINUTES
MAKES 35

185 g (6½ oz/1½ cups) plain (all-purpose) flour
60 g (2¼ oz/½ cup) unsweetened cocoa powder
115 g (4 oz/½ cup) caster (superfine) sugar
55 g (2 oz/½ cup) ground hazelnuts
100 g (3½ oz) unsalted butter, chopped
1 egg, at room temperature
100 g (3½ oz/⅓ cup) chocolate hazelnut spread,
at room temperature

METHOD
Grease two baking trays and line with baking paper.

Place the flour, cocoa, sugar and ground hazelnuts
in a food processor, add the butter and process for
30 seconds, or until the mixture resembles fine crumbs.
Add the egg and 1 tablespoon cold water to moisten.

Process until the mixture comes together. Turn the
dough onto a lightly floured surface and knead for
about 30 seconds, or until smooth.

Roll the dough out on a large sheet of baking paper,
to form a 25 x 35 cm (10 x 14 inch) rectangle. Trim
any uneven edges. Spread the hazelnut spread evenly
over the dough.

Using the paper to lift the dough, roll up from the
long side to form a log. Wrap tightly in the paper and
plastic wrap and refrigerate for 30 minutes. Preheat the
oven to 180°C (350°F/Gas 4).

Cut the dough into 1 cm (½ inch) slices. Place on the
baking trays, allowing room for spreading. Bake for
10–12 minutes, or until cooked through.

Transfer to a wire rack to cool.

FLORENTINES

PREPARATION 5 MINUTES
COOKING 15 MINUTES
MAKES 12

55 g (2 oz) unsalted butter
45 g (1½ oz/¼ cup) soft brown sugar
2 teaspoons honey
25 g (1 oz/¼ cup) roughly chopped flaked almonds
2 tablespoons chopped dried apricots
2 tablespoons chopped glacé cherries
2 tablespoons mixed peel
40 g (1½ oz/⅓ cup) plain (all-purpose) flour, sifted
110 g (3¾ oz/¾ cup) dark chocolate

METHOD
Preheat the oven to 180°C (350°F/Gas 4). Melt the
butter, sugar and honey in a saucepan until the butter
has melted and all the ingredients are combined.
Remove from the heat and add the almonds, apricots,
glacé cherries, mixed peel and the flour. Mix well.

Grease and line two baking trays with baking paper.
Place level tablespoons of the mixture on the trays,
allowing room for spreading. Reshape and flatten the
mixture into 5 cm (2 inch) rounds before cooking.

Bake for 10 minutes, or until lightly browned.
Cool on the trays, then allow to cool completely
on a wire rack.

To melt the chocolate, put the chocolate in a heatproof
bowl. Half fill a saucepan with water, bring to the
boil, then remove from the heat and sit the bowl over
the pan (don't let the bowl touch the water or the
chocolate will get too hot and seize). Stir occasionally
until the chocolate melts.

Spread the melted chocolate on the base of each
florentine and, using a fork, make a wavy pattern
in the chocolate before it sets. Let the chocolate set
completely before serving.

LIME AND WHITE CHOCOLATE FINGERS

PREPARATION 20 MINUTES
COOKING 15 MINUTES
MAKES 18

250 g (9 oz/2 cups) plain (all-purpose) flour
1 teaspoon baking powder
145 g (5 oz/⅔ cup) caster (superfine) sugar
75 g (2½ oz) unsalted butter, melted
2 tablespoons lime juice
grated zest from 2 limes
1 teaspoon vanilla extract
1 egg, at room temperature, lightly beaten
1 egg yolk, at room temperature
150 g (5½ oz/1 cup) chopped white chocolate

METHOD
Preheat the oven to 170°C (325°F/Gas 3). Lightly grease
and flour two baking trays.

Sift together the flour and baking powder and stir in
the sugar. Whisk together the butter, lime juice, zest,
vanilla, egg and egg yolk. Add the butter mixture to the
flour mixture and stir until a firm dough forms.

Take tablespoonfuls of the dough and, on a lightly
floured board, roll into thin logs 12 cm (4½ inches)
long. Put on the trays and bake for 10 minutes, or
until firm, swapping the position of the trays halfway
through cooking. Cool for 5 minutes, then transfer to
a wire rack to cool completely.

Put the chocolate in a small heatproof bowl. Sit the
bowl over a small saucepan of simmering water, stirring
frequently until the chocolate has melted. (Don't let
the bowl touch the water or the chocolate will get too
hot and seize.)

To decorate the fingers, place them close together
on the wire rack (put a piece of paper towel under
the rack to catch the drips) and, using a fork dipped into
the melted chocolate, drizzle the chocolate over
the top. Leave to set.

CHOCOLATE-FILLED SHORTBREADS

PREPARATION 30 MINUTES
COOKING 20 MINUTES
MAKES 20

125 g (4½ oz) unsalted butter, chopped, softened
60 g (2¼ oz/½ cup) icing (confectioners') sugar
1 teaspoon grated orange zest
125 g (4½ oz/1 cup) self-raising flour
60 g (2¼ oz/½ cup) cornflour (cornstarch)
1 tablespoon icing (confectioners') sugar, extra
1 tablespoon drinking chocolate

FILLING
60 g (2¼ oz/½ cup) roughly chopped dark chocolate
60 g (2¼ oz/¼ cup) cream cheese
1 egg, at room temperature, lightly beaten

METHOD
Preheat the oven to 180°C (350°F/Gas 4). Grease and
line two baking trays with baking paper.

Using electric beaters, beat the butter, icing sugar and
orange rind until light and creamy. Transfer to a food
processor and add the sifted flours and 1 tablespoon
iced water. Process for 20 seconds or until the mixture
comes together. Cover with plastic wrap and
refrigerate for 45 minutes.

To make the filling, put the chocolate in a heatproof bowl. Half fill a saucepan with water, bring to the boil, then remove from the heat and sit the bowl over the pan (don't let the bowl touch the water or the chocolate will get too hot and seize). Stir occasionally until the chocolate melts. Remove from the heat. Using electric beaters, beat the cream cheese until soft. Add the cooled chocolate and half the beaten egg. Mix well.

Roll out the shortbread mixture between two sheets of baking paper to a 3 mm ($\frac{1}{8}$ inch) thickness. Cut into 5 cm (2 inch) rounds using a fluted cutter. Place $\frac{1}{2}$ teaspoon of filling in the centre of half the rounds and brush the edges with the remaining beaten egg. Place the remaining rounds over the filling, and press the edges to seal. Put on the baking trays. Bake for 10–15 minutes, or until golden. Transfer to a wire rack.

To serve, dust the shortbreads with sifted icing sugar and drinking chocolate.

SULTANA AND CHOCOLATE CORNFLAKE COOKIES

PREPARATION 30 MINUTES
COOKING 15 MINUTES
MAKES 40

60 g (2¼ oz/⅓ cup) dark chocolate bits
60 g (2¼ oz/½ cup) sultanas
30 g (1 oz/¼ cup) roughly chopped walnuts
1 teaspoon grated orange zest
125 g (4½ oz) unsalted butter, chopped
80 g (2¾ oz/⅓ cup) caster (superfine) sugar
1 egg, at room temperature
125 g (4½ oz/1 cup) self-raising flour, sifted
80 g (2¾ oz/2⅔ cups) cornflakes, lightly crushed
80 g (2⅔ oz/½ cup) dark chocolate, melted

METHOD

Preheat the oven to 180°C (350°F/Gas 4). Lightly grease two baking trays.

Combine the chocolate bits, sultanas, walnuts and orange zest.

Using electric beaters, beat the butter and sugar until very light and creamy. Add the egg and beat well. Transfer to a large bowl. Using a metal spoon, fold in the flour. Add the sultana mixture and stir well.

Roll 2 level teaspoons of the mixture in the crushed cornflakes to coat. Bake for 15 minutes, or until golden and crisp. Transfer to a wire rack to cool. To serve, drizzle melted chocolate over the cooled cookies.

CHOCOLATE FUDGE SANDWICHES

PREPARATION 20 MINUTES
COOKING 30 MINUTES
MAKES 20–24

250 g (9 oz/2 cups) plain (all-purpose) flour
30 g (1 oz/¼ cup) unsweetened cocoa powder
200 g (7 oz) unsalted butter, chilled and diced
100 g (3½ oz) icing (confectioners') sugar
2 egg yolks, at room temperature, lightly beaten
1 teaspoon vanilla extract

FILLING
100 g (3½ oz/⅔ cup) chopped dark chocolate
1 tablespoon golden syrup or dark corn syrup
25 g (1 oz) unsalted butter, softened

METHOD
Preheat the oven to 200°C (400°F/Gas 6). Lightly
grease two baking trays.

Sift together the flour and cocoa and rub in the butter
until the mixture resembles fine breadcrumbs. Sift
in the icing sugar and mix well. Using a wooden
spoon, gradually stir in the egg yolks and vanilla
until a soft dough forms.

Transfer the dough to a lightly floured work surface and shape into a 4 x 6 x 26 cm (1½ x 2½ x 10½ inch) block. Wrap in plastic wrap and chill for 30 minutes, or until firm. Cut the dough into 40–48 slices, about 5 mm (¼ inch) wide. Place the slices on the baking trays, allowing room for spreading. Cooking in batches, bake for 10 minutes, or until firm. Cool on the trays for 5 minutes, then transfer to a wire rack to cool completely.

To make the filling, put the chocolate in a small heatproof bowl. Sit the bowl over a saucepan of simmering water. Don't let the bowl touch the water or the chocolate will get too hot and seize. Stir frequently until the chocolate has melted. Remove from the heat, stir in the golden syrup and butter and continue stirring until smooth.

Allow to cool a little, then put in the refrigerator and chill for 10 minutes, or until the mixture becomes a spreadable consistency. Use the chocolate filling to sandwich the biscuits together.

JAFFA TRIPLE-CHOC BROWNIES

PREPARATION 20 MINUTES
COOKING 45 MINUTES
MAKES 25 PIECES

125 g (4½ oz/ ½ cup) unsalted butter, cubed
350 g (12 oz/2⅓ cups) roughly chopped
dark chocolate
185 g (6½ oz/1 cup) soft brown sugar
3 eggs, at room temperature
2 teaspoons grated orange zest
125 g (4½ oz/1 cup) plain (all-purpose) flour
30 g (1 oz/¼ cup) unsweetened cocoa powder
100 g (3½ oz) milk chocolate bits
100 g (3½ oz) white chocolate bits

METHOD
Preheat the oven to 180°C (350°F/Gas 4).
Lightly grease a 23 cm (9 inch) square cake tin and line
with baking paper, leaving the paper hanging over on
two opposite sides.

Place the butter and 250 g (9 oz/1⅔ cups) of
the dark chocolate in a heatproof bowl. Half fill
a saucepan with water, bring to the boil, then remove
from the heat. Sit the bowl over the saucepan. Stir
occasionally until the butter and chocolate have
melted. Leave to cool.

Beat together the sugar, eggs and zest until thick
and fluffy. Fold in the chocolate.

Sift together the flour and cocoa, then stir into
the chocolate mixture.

Stir in the remaining dark chocolate and all the
chocolate bits. Spread into the tin and bake for
40 minutes, or until just cooked. Cool in the tin before
lifting out, using the paper as handles.

Cut into squares. To serve, drizzle with melted dark
chocolate, if desired.

WHITE CHOCOLATE, LEMON AND MACADAMIA BISCOTTI

PREPARATION 20 MINUTES
COOKING 20 MINUTES
MAKES 70

180 g (6½ oz) unsalted butter, melted and cooled
230 g (8 oz/1 cup) caster (superfine) sugar
3 eggs, at room temperature
grated zest from 3 lemons
1 teaspoon vanilla extract
200 g (7 oz/1⅓ cups) chopped white chocolate
120 g (4¼ oz) macadamia halves
375 g (1 lb/3 cups) plain (all-purpose) flour
1 teaspoon baking powder

METHOD
Preheat the oven to 160°C (315°F/Gas 2). Line two
baking trays with baking paper.

Whisk together the melted butter, sugar, eggs, lemon
zest and vanilla. Stir in the chocolate and macadamias.

Sift together the flour and baking powder. Add to the
butter and chocolate mixture and use a wooden spoon
to stir to a soft dough (it will be slightly sticky).
Divide into four equal portions. On a floured surface,
shape each portion into a log about 5 cm (2 inches)
wide and 20 cm (8 inches) long. Place on lined trays,
allowing room for spreading at least 7 cm (3 inches)
between each. Slightly flatten each log to about
7 cm (3 inches) wide and 24 cm (9½ inches) long.

Bake for 30–35 minutes or the until logs are firm to
touch and are just cooked through. Cool on the trays.

Reduce the oven to 150°C (300°F/Gas 2). Use a sharp
knife to cut two of the logs diagonally into 1 cm
(½ inch) thick slices. Place on a lined baking tray in a
single layer. Bake for 20 minutes or until the biscotti
are crisp. Cool on the tray, then transfer the biscotti
to a wire rack. Repeat with the remaining two logs.

CHOCOLATE AND GLACE CHERRY SLICE

PREPARATION 25 MINUTES
COOKING 25 MINUTES
MAKES 28

125 g (4½ oz/1 cup) plain (all-purpose) flour
40 g (1½ oz/⅓ cup) unsweetened cocoa powder
80 g (2¾ oz/⅓ cup) caster (superfine) sugar
125 g (4½ oz) unsalted butter, melted
1 teaspoon vanilla extract
480 g (15 oz/2 cups) finely chopped glacé cherries
60 g (2¼ oz/½ cup) icing (confectioners') sugar
135 g (4¾ oz/1½ cups) desiccated coconut
125 ml (4 fl oz/½ cup) sweetened condensed milk
60 g (2¼ oz) unsalted butter, extra, melted
50 g (1¾ oz) Copha (white vegetable
shortening), melted
150 g (5½ oz) dark cooking chocolate
25 g (1 oz) unsalted butter, extra

METHOD

Preheat the oven to 180°C (350°F/Gas 4). Lightly grease an 18 x 27 cm (7 x 10½ inch) baking tin and line with baking paper, leaving the paper hanging over the two long sides.

Sift together the flour and cocoa into a bowl, add the sugar, butter and vanilla, then mix to form a dough. Gather the mixture and turn onto a well-floured surface. Knead for 1 minute, then press into the base of the tin. Chill for 20 minutes. Cover with baking paper and baking beads and bake for 10–15 minutes. Remove the paper and beads and bake for a further 5 minutes. Allow to cool to room temperature.

Combine the cherries, icing sugar and coconut. Stir in the condensed milk, extra butter and Copha, then spread over the base. Chill for about 30 minutes.

Chop the chocolate and extra butter into small even-sized pieces and place in a heatproof bowl. Bring a saucepan of water to the boil and remove from the heat. Sit the bowl over the pan, (don't let the bowl touch the water or the chocolate will get too hot and seize). Allow to stand, stirring occasionally, until melted. Pour over the cooled cherry mixture, then chill until set. Cut into squares and serve.

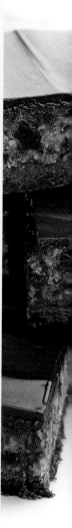

CHOCOLATE PEANUT SLICE

PREPARATION 35 MINUTES
COOKING 20 MINUTES
SERVES 8–10

250 g (9 oz) finely crushed chocolate chip cookies
130 g (4½ oz) unsalted butter, melted
45 g (1½ oz/¼ cup) soft brown sugar
2 eggs, at room temperature
60 ml (2 fl oz/¼ cup) sweetened condensed milk
250 g (9 oz/1 cup) smooth peanut butter
150 g (5½ oz/1 cup) chopped dark chocolate, melted
2 tablespoons unsweetened cocoa powder

METHOD
Preheat the oven to 180°C (350°F/Gas 4).
Line a 28 x 18 cm (11 x 7 inch) tin with enough
baking paper to extend over the longest sides.

Combine the cookie crumbs and half the melted butter. Press firmly into base of the tin. Refrigerate for 10–15 minutes, or until the mixture is firm.

Using electric beaters, beat the rest of butter and sugar until light and creamy. Add the eggs, condensed milk and peanut butter and mix until smooth. Spread evenly over the biscuit base. Bake for 15–20 minutes, or until lightly golden. Leave in the tin to cool.

Spread the melted chocolate over the cooled slice. Allow the chocolate to set, then remove from the tin. Cut into bars and serve.

CHOCOLATE CHEESECAKE SLICE

PREPARATION 40 MINUTES
COOKING 45 MINUTES
SERVES 8–10

200 g (7 oz/1½ cups) plain chocolate cookie crumbs
80 g (2¾ oz) unsalted butter, melted
100 g (3½ oz) chocolate bits

FILLING
375 g (13 oz) cream cheese, softened
115 g (4 oz/½ cup) caster (superfine) sugar
3 eggs, at room temperature
150 g (5½ oz/1 cup) chopped white chocolate, melted

TOPPING
150 g (5½ oz/1 cup) chopped white chocolate, melted
160 g (5¾ oz/⅔ cup) sour cream

METHOD

Preheat the oven to 180°C (350°F/Gas 4). Grease
a 20 x 30 cm (8 x 12 inch) cake tin and line with
baking paper, allowing the paper to hang over the
longer sides.

Combine the crumbs and butter. Press into the base
of the tin. Sprinkle evenly with the chocolate bits.

To make the filling, use electric beaters to beat the
cream cheese until creamy. Beat in the sugar until
smooth. Add the eggs one at a time, beating well after
each addition. Put the white chocolate in a heatproof
bowl. Half fill a saucepan with water, bring to the
boil, then remove from the heat and sit the bowl over
the pan (don't let the bowl touch the water or the
chocolate will get too hot and seize). Stir occasionally
until the chocolate melts. Add the chocolate to the
cream cheese mixture and beat until smooth. Spread
over the base. Bake for 30 minutes, or until just set.
Cool, cover and refrigerate until firm.

To make the topping, combine the chocolate and sour
cream in a heatproof bowl. Sit the bowl over a pan of
simmering water. Stir until the chocolate has melted
and the mixture is smooth. Remove from the heat.

Spread evenly over the cheesecake, marking regular
lines with a flat-bladed knife. Refrigerate until firm.
Cut into slices and serve.

CHOCOLATE, BLACKBERRY AND COCONUT SLICE

PREPARATION 15 MINUTES
COOKING 55 MINUTES
MAKES 25 PIECES

80 g (6 oz/2 cups) desiccated coconut
125 g (10½ oz/2 cups) plain (all-purpose) flour, sifted
165 g (5¾ oz/¾ cup firmly packed) soft brown sugar
200 g (7 oz/1⅓ cups) chopped dark chocolate
100 g (3½ oz) unsalted butter, chopped
2 eggs, at room temperature, lightly beaten
160 g (5½ oz/½ cup) blackberry jam
icing (confectioners') sugar, to dust

METHOD

Preheat the oven to 170°C (325°F/Gas 3). Line the base and sides of a 20 cm (8 inch) square cake tin with two strips of baking paper.

Combine the coconut, flour and sugar. Set aside.

Put the chocolate and butter in a small saucepan over low heat, stirring frequently, until the chocolate and butter just melt and the mixture is smooth. Add to the coconut mixture with the eggs and use a wooden spoon to mix well.

Spoon half the chocolate mixture into the tin and press firmly and evenly into the tin. Spread the jam evenly over the chocolate mixture. Top with the remaining mixture, pressing with the back of the spoon to cover the jam and smooth the surface.

Bake for 50 minutes, or until a skewer comes out clean when poked into the centre. Cool in the tin for 10 minutes before using the baking paper to transfer the slice to a wire rack. Cool completely.

Cut into 4 cm (1½ inch) squares and serve dusted with icing sugar.

WALNUT AND FIG HEDGEHOG BARS

PREPARATION 15 MINUTES
COOKING 5 MINUTES
MAKES 20

100 g (3½ oz) broken pieces shredded wheat biscuits
115 g (4 oz/⅔ cup) chopped dried figs
50 g (1¾ oz/½ cup) walnut halves, coarsely chopped
300 g (10½ oz/2 cups) chopped dark chocolate
60 g (2¼ oz) unsalted butter, chopped
90 g (3¼ oz/¼ cup) honey

METHOD
Line the base and sides of an 18 cm (7 inch) square
cake tin with two strips of baking paper.

Combine the biscuits, figs and walnuts. Combine the
chocolate, butter and honey in a small saucepan over
low heat. Stir frequently, until the chocolate and butter
have melted and the mixture is smooth. Add to
the biscuit and fruit mixture and mix well. Spoon
evenly into the tin. Tap the tin gently on the bench
to settle the mixture.

Cover with plastic wrap and place in the fridge for
1 hour or until firm. Remove from the tin and cut into
2.5 x 6 cm (1 x 2½ inch) bars and serve.

CHOCOLATE CARAMEL SLICE

PREPARATION 15 MINUTES
COOKING 20 MINUTES
MAKES 24

200 g (7 oz) crushed plain chocolate cookies
100 g (3½ oz) unsalted butter, melted
2 tablespoons desiccated coconut
125 g (4½ oz) unsalted butter, extra
400 ml (14 fl oz) tin sweetened condensed milk
80 g (2¾ oz/⅓ cup) caster (superfine) sugar
3 tablespoons maple syrup
250 g (9 oz) dark chocolate
2 teaspoons oil

METHOD
Grease a 30 x 20 cm (12 x 8 inch) baking tin and
line with baking paper, leaving it hanging over the
two long sides.

Combine the cookies, melted butter and coconut,
then press into the tin and smooth the surface.

Combine the butter, condensed milk, sugar and maple
syrup in a small saucepan. Stir over low heat for
15 minutes, or until the sugar has dissolved and the
mixture is smooth, thick and lightly coloured. Remove
from the heat and cool slightly. Pour the caramel
over the base of the slice and smooth the surface.
Refrigerate for 30 minutes, or until firm.

Chop the chocolate into small bite-sized pieces.
Put the chocolate in a heatproof bowl. Half fill a
saucepan with water, bring to the boil, then remove
from the heat and sit the bowl over the pan (don't
let the bowl touch the water or the chocolate will
get too hot and seize). Allow to stand, stirring
occasionally, until the chocolate has melted.
Add the oil and stir until smooth. Spread over the
caramel and leave until partially set before marking
into 24 triangles. Refrigerate until firm. When the
slice has set, cut into triangles.

LAMINGTONS

PREPARATION 40 MINUTES
COOKING 20 MINUTES
MAKES 60

4 eggs, at room temperature, separated
145 g (5 oz/⅔ cup) caster (superfine) sugar
2 tablespoons unsweetened cocoa powder
30 g (1 oz/¼ cup) plain (all-purpose) flour
30 g (1 oz/¼ cup) cornflour (cornstarch)
40 g (1½ oz/⅓ cup) self-raising flour

CHOCOLATE ICING
375 g (1 lb/3 cups) icing (confectioners') sugar
60 g (2¼ oz/½ cup) unsweetened cocoa powder
90 g (3¼ oz) butter, chopped
1 tablespoon instant coffee powder
270 g (9½ oz/3 cups) desiccated coconut

METHOD

Preheat the oven to 180°C (350°F/Gas 4). Line a
20 x 30 cm (8 x 12 inch) cake tin with baking paper.

Using electric beaters, beat the egg whites until soft
peaks form. Add the sugar gradually, beating well
after each addition. Beat until the sugar dissolves
and the mixture is thick and glossy. Add the egg yolks
and beat well. Gently fold through the sifted
cocoa and flours.

Pour into the tin and smooth the surface. Bake for
20 minutes, or until the cake is springy to the touch.
Stand in the tin for 5 minutes before turning out onto
a wire rack to cool. Cut into 3 cm (1¼ inch) squares.

To make the chocolate icing, sift together the icing
sugar and cocoa. Stir in the butter, 185 ml (6 fl oz/
¾ cup) boiling water and the coffee. Mix until smooth.
Place the coconut on a large plate. Using two forks,
dip the cake squares, one at a time, into the chocolate
icing, toss in coconut and then place on a wire rack.
Repeat until all the cake squares have been coated.
Allow to stand at least 1 hour before serving.

DESSERTS
AND
CAKES

FLOURLESS CHOCOLATE CAKE

PREPARATION 20 MINUTES
COOKING 1 HOUR
SERVES 10

500 g (1 lb 2 oz/3⅓ cups) chopped dark chocolate
6 eggs, at room temperature
2 tablespoons Frangelico or brandy
165 g (5¾ oz/1½ cups) ground hazelnuts
250 ml (9 fl oz/1 cup) cream, whipped
icing (confectioners') sugar and cream, to serve

METHOD
Preheat the oven to 150°C (300°F/Gas 2). Grease
a 20 cm (8 inch) round cake tin and line the base
with baking paper.

Put the chocolate in a heatproof bowl. Half fill
a saucepan with water, bring to the boil, then remove
from the heat and sit the bowl over the pan (don't
let the bowl touch the water or the chocolate will
get too hot and seize). Stir occasionally until
the chocolate melts.

Put the eggs in a heatproof bowl and add
the Frangelico. Put the bowl over a pan of barely
simmering water — don't let it touch the water.
Beat the eggs with electric beaters on high speed
for 7 minutes, or until light and foamy.
Remove from the heat.

Using a metal spoon, quickly and lightly fold the
chocolate and ground hazelnuts into the eggs. Fold in
the whipped cream and pour the mixture into the cake
tin. Put the cake tin in a roasting tin and pour enough
boiling water into the roasting tin to come halfway
up the side of the cake tin. Bake for 1 hour, or until a
skewer comes out clean when poked into the centre
of the cake. Remove the cake tin from the water bath
and cool to room temperature. Cover with plastic
wrap and refrigerate overnight.

Turn out the cake onto a plate, remove the
paper and cut into slices. Dust with icing sugar
and serve with cream.

MARBLE CAKE

PREPARATION 20 MINUTES
COOKING 1 HOUR
SERVES 6

1 vanilla bean or 1 teaspoon vanilla extract
185 g (6½ oz) chopped unsalted butter, softened
30 g (8 oz/1 cup) caster (superfine) sugar
3 eggs, at room temperature
280 g (10 oz/2¼ cups) self-raising flour
185 ml (6 fl oz/¾ cup) milk
2 tablespoons unsweetened cocoa powder
1½ tablespoons warm milk

METHOD
Preheat the oven to 200°C (400°F/Gas 6). Lightly
grease a 25 x 11 x 7.5 cm (10 x 4¼ x 3 inch) loaf
(bar) tin and line the base with baking paper.

Split the vanilla bean down the middle and scrape out
the seeds. Put the seeds (or vanilla extract) in a bowl
with the butter and sugar and, using electric beaters,
cream the mixture until pale and fluffy.

Add the eggs one at a time, beating well after each addition. Sift the flour, then fold it into the creamed mixture alternately with the milk until they are combined. Put half the mixture into another bowl.

Mix the cocoa and warm milk until smooth, then add to one of the bowls and mix well. Spoon the plain mixture and chocolate mixture into the tin in alternating spoonfuls. Use a metal skewer to gently cut through the mixture a few times to create a marbled effect. Bake for 50–60 minutes, or until a skewer comes out clean when poked into the centre of the cake. Leave in the tin for 5 minutes before turning out onto a wire rack to cool. Cut into slices and serve.

WALNUT AND CHOCOLATE PLUM TORTE

PREPARATION 30 MINUTES
COOKING 1 HOUR 10 MINUTES
SERVES 8–10

200 g (7 oz/2 cups) walnuts
200 g (7 oz/1⅓ cups) chopped dark chocolate
2 teaspoons instant coffee granules
100 g (3½ oz/heaped ¾ cup) cornflour (cornstarch)
200 g (7 oz) unsalted butter, softened
185 g (6½ oz/1 cup) raw caster (superfine) sugar
4 eggs, at room temperature, separated
2 teaspoons coffee liqueur
450 g (1 lb) small firm plums (angelina or sugar plums
are ideal) or 800 g (1 lb 12 oz) medium to large plums,
halved and stoned
2 tablespoons dark brown sugar
20 g (¾ oz) unsalted butter, extra
vanilla ice cream or whipped cream, to serve

METHOD

Preheat the oven to 170°C (325°F/Gas 3). Grease a
25 cm (10 inch) spring-form cake tin and line the base
with baking paper.

In a food processor, grind the walnuts and chocolate
until finely processed. Add the coffee granules and
cornflour and process briefly.

Cream the butter and sugar with electric beaters until
pale. Add the egg yolks, one at a time, alternating
with some of the walnut mixture. Beat well after each
addition. Stir in the liqueur.

Whisk the egg whites until soft peaks form. Fold a
large spoonful into the walnut mixture, then gently
fold the rest of the egg white through. Spoon into the
tin and smooth the surface. Bake for 30 minutes.

Remove from the oven and arrange the plums, cut
side up, on top of the cake. Scatter the brown sugar
over the plums and dot the extra butter over the sugar.
Return the torte to the oven and bake for another
40 minutes, or until a skewer comes out clean when
poked into the centre.

Remove the torte from the oven and cool for 1 minute,
then carefully run a knife around the edge to prevent
any toffee sticking to the tin. Leave in the tin for
15 minutes before turning out onto a wire rack.
Serve warm in slices, accompanied with softened
vanilla ice cream or whipped cream.

CHOCOLATE RUM AND RAISIN CAKE

PREPARATION 20 MINUTES
COOKING 1 HOUR 5 MINUTES
SERVES 8–10

2 tablespoons dark rum
40 g (1½ oz/¼ cup) chopped raisins
220 g (7¾ oz/1⅓ cups) self-raising flour
40 g (1½ oz/⅓ cup) plain (all-purpose) flour
40 g (1½ oz/⅓ cup) unsweetened cocoa powder
170 g (6 oz/¾ cup) caster (superfine) sugar
55 g (2 oz/¼ cup) raw (demerara) sugar
200 g (7 oz) unsalted butter
1 tablespoon golden syrup
100 g (3½ oz/⅔ cup) chopped dark chocolate
2 eggs, at room temperature, lightly beaten
icing (confectioners') sugar and unsweetened
cocoa powder, to serve
cream, to serve

METHOD

Preheat the oven to 150°C (300°F/Gas 2). Brush a
20 cm (8 inch) round cake tin with melted butter or oil.
Line the base and side of the tin with baking paper.

Combine 60 ml (2 fl oz/¼ cup) water, the rum
and raisins in a small bowl and set aside. In a separate
bowl, sift the flours and cocoa and make a well
in the centre.

Combine the sugars, butter, golden syrup and
chocolate in a saucepan. Stir over low heat until the
butter and chocolate have melted and the sugar has
dissolved, then remove from the heat. Stir in the
raisin and rum mixture.

Using a metal spoon, fold the butter and chocolate
mixture into the well. Add the eggs and mix well until
smooth. Pour into the tin and smooth the surface.
Bake for 1 hour, or until a skewer comes out clean
when poked into the centre of the cake. Leave in the
tin for 1 hour before turning out onto a wire rack.
Dust with sifted cocoa and icing sugar. Cut the cake
into wedges and serve warm with cream.

RICH CHOCOLATE AND WHISKY
MUD CAKE WITH SUGARED VIOLETS

PREPARATION 40 MINUTES
COOKING 1 HOUR 25 MINUTES
SERVES 8–10

250 g (9 oz) unsalted butter, cubed
200 g (7 oz/1⅓ cups) chopped dark chocolate
375 g (13 oz/1⅔ cups) caster (superfine) sugar
125 ml (4 fl oz/½ cup) whisky
1 tablespoon instant coffee granules
185 g (6½ oz/1½ cups) plain (all-purpose) flour
60 g (2¼ oz/½ cup) self-raising flour
40 g (1½ oz/⅓ cup) unsweetened cocoa powder
2 eggs, at room temperature, lightly beaten

CHOCOLATE GLAZE
80 ml (2½ fl oz/⅓ cup) cream
90 g (3¼ oz/scant ⅔ cup) chopped dark chocolate

sugared violets and silver cachous, to decorate

METHOD
Preheat the oven to 160°C (315°F/Gas 2–3). Grease
a 20 cm (8 inch) square tin and line the base and sides
with baking paper.

Put the butter, chocolate, sugar and whisky in a saucepan. Dissolve the coffee granules in 125 ml (4 fl oz/½ cup) hot water and add to the mixture. Stir over low heat until melted and smooth.

Sift the flours and cocoa into a large bowl, then pour in the butter mixture and whisk together. Whisk in the eggs and pour into the tin.

Bake for about 1 hour 15 minutes, or until a skewer comes out clean when poked into the centre of the cake. Pour the extra whisky over the cake. Leave in the tin for 20 minutes before turning out onto a wire rack, placed over a baking tray, to cool.

To make the chocolate glaze, put the cream in a small saucepan and bring just to the boil. Remove from the heat and add the chocolate. Stir until melted and smooth. Set aside to cool and thicken a little. Spread the glaze over the cake, allowing it to drizzle over the sides. Leave the glaze to set. Decorate with the sugared violets and silver cachous.

CHOCOLATE FRENCH TOAST

PREPARATION 20 MINUTES
COOKING 10 MINUTES
SERVES 2

50 g (1¾ oz/1/3 cup) chopped dark chocolate
4 slices day-old brioche 1.5 cm (⅝ inch) thick,
or 4 slices cob or cottage loaf
1 egg, at room temperature
1½ tablespoons cream
1½ tablespoons milk
1 tablespoon caster (superfine) sugar
½ teaspoon vanilla extract
¼ teaspoon ground cinnamon
20 g (¾ oz) unsalted butter
icing (confectioners') sugar, to dust

METHOD
Place the chocolate in a small heatproof bowl
over a saucepan of simmering water, (don't let the
bowl touch the water or the chocolate will get too
hot and seize). Stir frequently until the chocolate just
melts and the mixture is smooth. Remove the bowl
from the saucepan.

Spread two slices of brioche (or cob or cottage loaf) with the melted chocolate and sandwich together, repeat with the remaining slices.

Use a fork to whisk the egg, cream, milk, sugar, vanilla and cinnamon in a wide bowl.

Place the sandwiches in the egg mixture, allowing the bread to soak it up (allow about 30 seconds each side). Meanwhile, melt the butter in a frying pan over medium heat.

When the butter is sizzling, remove the sandwiches from the bowl, allowing any excess egg mixture to drain off, and add to the pan. Cook for 2 minutes each side, or until well browned.

Cut the sandwiches in half and serve, dusted with icing sugar.

CHOCOLATE CREPES WITH GRAND MARNIER SAUCE

PREPARATION 40 MINUTES
COOKING 20 MINUTES
MAKES 8–10

2 eggs, at room temperature
2 tablespoons caster (superfine) sugar
60 g (2¼ oz/½ cup) plain (all-purpose) flour
1 tablespoon unsweetened cocoa powder
250 ml (9 fl oz/1 cup) milk
3 oranges
125 g (4½ oz/½ cup) sour cream or crème fraîche
75 g (2½ oz/½ cup) grated white chocolate
250 g (9 oz) blueberries

SAUCE
180 g (6½ oz/1¼ cups) chopped dark chocolate
185 ml (6 fl oz/¾ cup) cream
2–3 tablespoons Grand Marnier

METHOD
Whisk the eggs and sugar in a large jug. Gradually
whisk in the sifted flour and cocoa, alternately with
the milk, until the batter is free of lumps. Cover with
plastic wrap and set aside for 30 minutes.

Cut a 1 cm (½ inch) slice from the ends of each orange. Cut the skin away in a circular motion, cutting only deep enough to remove all the white membrane and skin. Cut the flesh into segments between each membrane. (Do this over a bowl to catch any juice.) Place the segments in the bowl with the juice. Cover with plastic wrap and refrigerate.

Heat a 20 cm (8 inch) frying pan over medium heat. Brush lightly with a little melted butter. Pour 2–3 tablespoons of crepe batter into the pan and swirl evenly over the base. Cook over medium heat for 1 minute or until the underside is cooked. Turn the crepe over and cook the other side. Transfer the crepe to a plate and cover with a tea towel (dish towel) to keep warm. Continue making crepes until you use all the batter. (This mixture should make 8–10 crepes, depending on their thickness.)

To make the sauce, drain the oranges, reserving the juice. Put the juice in a saucepan with the chocolate, cream and Grand Marnier. Stir over low heat until the chocolate has melted and the mixture is smooth.

To assemble the crepes, place 1 heaped teaspoon of sour cream on a quarter of each crepe. Sprinkle with the grated white chocolate. Fold the crepe in half, and in half again to make a wedge shape. Place two crepes on each serving plate. Spoon the warm sauce over the crepes and serve with orange segments and blueberries.

MOLTEN CHOCOLATE PUDDINGS

PREPARATION 20 MINUTES
COOKING 20 MINUTES
SERVES 6

200 g (7 oz/1⅓ cups) chopped dark chocolate
100 g (3½ oz) unsalted butter, cubed
2 eggs, at room temperature
2 egg yolks, at room temperature
55 g (2 oz/¼ cup) caster (superfine) sugar
2 tablespoons plain (all-purpose) flour, sifted
unsweetened cocoa powder, to dust

MALT CREAM
200 ml (7 fl oz) cream, for whipping
45 g (1½ oz/⅓ cup) malted milk powder
1 tablespoon icing (confectioners') sugar, sifted

METHOD
Preheat the oven to 180°C (350°F/Gas 4). Brush six
185 ml (6 fl oz/¾ cup) ramekins with melted butter.
Place on a baking tray.

Combine the chocolate and butter in a small saucepan over low heat. Stir frequently until the chocolate and butter have melted and the mixture is smooth. Remove from the heat.

Beat the whole eggs, egg yolks and sugar with electric beaters until thick and pale. Add the chocolate mixture and flour and use a large metal spoon or spatula to fold in until evenly combined.

Divide the mixture evenly among the ramekins. Bake for 12 minutes, or until the puddings have risen almost to the top of the ramekins (they will still look slightly underdone).

Meanwhile, to make the malt cream, whisk the cream, malted milk powder and icing sugar until soft peaks form. Cover and place in the fridge.

Turn the puddings out onto serving plates, dust with the cocoa powder and serve with the malt cream.

CHOCOLATE SOUFFLES

PREPARATION 20 MINUTES
COOKING 20 MINUTES
SERVES 6

180 g (6½ oz/1¼ cups) chopped dark chocolate
5 eggs, at room temperature, separated
55 g (2 oz/¼ cup) caster (superfine) sugar
2 egg whites,
extra icing (confectioners') sugar, for dusting

METHOD
Preheat the oven to 200°C (400°F/Gas 6) and put
a baking tray into the oven to warm.

Wrap a double layer of baking paper around the
outside of six 250 ml (9 fl oz/1 cup) ramekins to come
about 3 cm (1¼ inches) above the rim, and secure
with string. This encourages the soufflé to rise well.
Brush the insides of the ramekins with melted butter
and sprinkle with a little caster sugar, shaking to coat
evenly and tipping out any excess. This layer of butter
and sugar helps the soufflé to grip the sides and rise
as it cooks.

Place the chocolate in a heatproof bowl set over a saucepan of simmering water. Don't let the bowl touch the water, or the chocolate will get too hot and seize. Stir until the chocolate is melted and smooth, then remove from the heat. Stir in the egg yolks and caster sugar.

Beat the 7 egg whites until stiff peaks form. Gently fold one-third of the egg whites into the chocolate mixture to loosen it. Then, using a metal spoon, fold in the remaining egg whites until just combined.

Spoon the mixture into the ramekins and run your thumb or a blunt knife around the inside rim of the dish and the edge of the mixture. This ridge helps the soufflé to rise evenly. Place on the heated baking tray and bake for 12–15 minutes, or until well risen and just set. Do not open the oven door while the soufflés are baking.

Cut the string and remove the paper collars. Serve immediately, lightly dusted with sifted icing sugar.

CHOCOLATE AND CINNAMON
SELF-SAUCING PUDDINGS

PREPARATION 20 MINUTES
COOKING 50 MINUTES
SERVES 4

50 g (1¾ oz/⅓ cup) chopped dark chocolate
60 g (2¼ oz) unsalted butter, cubed
2 tablespoons unsweetened cocoa powder, sifted
170 ml (5¼ fl oz/⅔ cup) milk
125 g (4½ oz/1 cup) self-raising flour
115 g (4 oz/½ cup) caster (superfine) sugar
80 g (2¾ oz/⅓ cup firmly packed) soft brown sugar
1 egg, at room temperature, lightly beaten

CINNAMON SAUCE
1½ teaspoons ground cinnamon
50 g (1¾ oz) unsalted butter, cubed
60 g (2¼ oz/¼ cup firmly packed) soft brown sugar
30 g (1 oz/¼ cup) unsweetened cocoa powder, sifted

METHOD

Preheat the oven to 180°C (350°F/Gas 4). Grease four 250 ml (9 fl oz/1 cup) ramekins.

Combine the chocolate, butter, cocoa and milk in a saucepan. Stir over low heat until the chocolate has melted. Remove from the heat.

Sift the flour into a large bowl and stir in the sugars. Add to the chocolate mixture with the egg and mix well. Spoon into the ramekins, put on a baking tray and set aside while you make the sauce.

To make the cinnamon sauce, combine the cinnamon, butter, brown sugar, cocoa and 375 ml (13 fl oz/ 1½ cups) water in a saucepan. Stir over low heat until combined. Carefully pour the sauce onto the puddings over the back of a spoon. Bake for 40 minutes, or until firm. Serve warm with thick cream or ice cream.

CHOCOLATE CHIP PANCAKES WITH HOT FUDGE SAUCE

PREPARATION 35 MINUTES
COOKING 30 MINUTES
MAKES 16

250 g (9 oz/2 cups) self-raising flour
2 tablespoons unsweetened cocoa powder
1 teaspoon bicarbonate of soda (baking soda)
55 g (2 oz/¼ cup) caster (superfine) sugar
130 g (4½ oz/¾ cup) dark chocolate bits
250 ml (9 fl oz/1 cup) milk
250 ml (9 fl oz/1 cup) cream
2 eggs, at room temperature, lightly beaten
30 g (1 oz) unsalted butter, melted
3 egg whites, at room temperature
whipped cream or ice cream, to serve
icing (confectioners') sugar, to dust

HOT FUDGE SAUCE
150 g (5½ oz/1 cup) chopped dark chocolate
30 g (1 oz) unsalted butter
2 tablespoons light corn syrup
95 g (3¼ oz/½ cup) soft brown sugar
125 ml (4 fl oz/½ cup) pouring cream

METHOD

Sift the flour, cocoa and bicarbonate of soda into
a bowl. Stir in the sugar and chocolate bits and make
a well in the centre. Whisk the milk, cream, eggs
and melted butter in a jug, then gradually pour into
the well and stir until just combined. Cover and set
aside for 15 minutes.

Beat the egg whites until soft peaks form. Using a large
metal spoon, stir a heaped tablespoon of the beaten
egg white into the batter to loosen it up, then lightly
fold in the remaining egg white.

Heat a frying pan and brush lightly with melted
butter or oil. Pour 60 ml (2 fl oz/¼ cup) of batter
into the pan and cook over medium heat until the
underside is browned.

Flip the pancake over and cook the other side.
Transfer to a plate, and cover with a tea towel while
cooking the remaining batter. Stack between sheets of
baking paper to prevent the pancakes sticking together.

To make the hot fudge sauce, put all the ingredients
in a saucepan and stir over low heat until melted and
smooth. Dust the pancakes with icing sugar and serve
warm with whipped cream or ice cream and drizzled
with hot fudge sauce.

CHOCOLATE FUDGE PUDDINGS

PREPARATION 20 MINUTES
COOKING 45 MINUTES
SERVES 8

160 g (5½ oz) unsalted butter, softened
170 g (6 oz/¾ cup) caster (superfine) sugar
100 g (3½ oz) chocolate, melted and cooled
2 eggs, at room temperature
60 g (2¼ oz/½ cup) plain (all-purpose) flour
125 g (4½ oz/1 cup) self-raising flour
30 g (1 oz/¼ cup) unsweetened cocoa powder
1 teaspoon bicarbonate of soda (baking soda)
125 ml (4 fl oz/½ cup) milk
whipped cream, to serve

SAUCE
60 g (2¼ oz) unsalted butter, chopped
115 g (4 oz) chocolate, chopped
125 ml (4 fl oz/½ cup) cream
1 teaspoon vanilla extract

METHOD
Preheat the oven to 180°C (350°F/Gas 4).
Lightly grease eight 250 ml (9 fl oz/1 cup) ramekins
with melted butter and line the bases with rounds
of baking paper.

Beat the butter and sugar until light and creamy.
Add the melted chocolate, beating well. Add the eggs
one at a time, beating well after each addition.

Sift together the flours, cocoa and bicarbonate of soda,
then fold into the chocolate. Add the milk and fold
through. Pour into the ramekins until they are half full.

Cover the ramekins with buttered foil and place in a
roasting tin. Pour enough boiling water into the tin
to come halfway up the sides of the ramekins. Bake
for 35–40 minutes, or until a skewer comes out clean
when poked into the centre of a pudding.

To make the sauce, combine the butter, chocolate,
cream and vanilla in a saucepan. Stir over low heat
until the butter and chocolate have completely melted.
Pour over the pudding and serve with whipped cream.

CHOCOLATE RUM FONDUE

PREPARATION 15 MINUTES
COOKING 10 MINUTES
SERVES 6

250 g (9 oz/1⅔ cups) chopped dark chocolate
125 ml (4 fl oz/½ cup) cream
1–2 tablespoons rum
1 mandarin, tangerine or small orange, peeled,
divided into segments
2 figs, quartered lengthways
250 g (9 oz/1⅔ cups) strawberries, hulled
250 g (9 oz/2¾ cups) white marshmallows

METHOD
Melt the chocolate and cream in a heatproof bowl
over a saucepan of simmering water. Stir until smooth,
remove the bowl from the heat and stir in the rum, to
taste. Pour while still warm into the fondue pot.

Arrange the fruit and marshmallows on a serving
platter. Serve with forks to dip the fruit into
the chocolate fondue.

CHOCOLATE AND ALMOND PEAR PUDDINGS

PREPARATION 20 MINUTES
COOKING 25 MINUTES
SERVES 8

115 g (4 oz/⅓ cup) golden syrup
8 tinned pear halves in natural juice, drained
60 g (2¼ oz/½ cup) plain (all-purpose) flour
30 g (1 oz/¼ cup) unsweetened cocoa powder
2 teaspoons baking powder
1 teaspoon ground allspice (optional)
55 g (2 oz/½ cup) ground almonds
3 eggs, at room temperature
165 g (5¾ oz/¾ cup firmly packed) soft brown sugar
60 ml (2 fl oz/¼ cup) milk
115 g (4 oz/⅓ cup) golden syrup, extra warmed
slightly, to serve
vanilla ice cream or cream, to serve

METHOD

Preheat the oven to 180°C (350°F/Gas 4). Brush eight holes of a 12-hole muffin tray with melted butter to grease, and line the base with rounds of baking paper. Divide the golden syrup evenly among the eight muffin holes to cover the bases. Place a pear half, cut side down, in each.

Sift together the flour, cocoa, baking powder and allspice, if using. Stir in the ground almonds.

Use an electric beater with a whisk attachment to whisk the eggs and sugar until thick and pale. Pour in the milk, add the flour mixture and use a metal spoon to fold together.

Spoon the cake mixture evenly over the pears. Bake for 25 minutes, or until a skewer comes out clean when poked into the centre of a pudding. Stand for 3 minutes before turning out onto a wire rack. Immediately remove the baking paper and transfer the puddings to serving plates. Drizzle with extra golden syrup and serve with cream or ice cream.

BAKED CHOCOLATE CUSTARDS

PREPARATION 20 MINUTES
COOKING 40 MINUTES
SERVES 10

30 g (1 oz) unsalted butter, melted
55 g (2 oz/¼ cup) caster (superfine) sugar, for dusting
300 ml (10½ fl oz) cream
200 ml (7 fl oz) milk
200 g (7 oz/1⅓ cups) roughly chopped dark chocolate
grated zest of 1 orange
6 eggs, at room temperature
115 g (4 oz/½ cup) caster (superfine) sugar
extra raspberries, to serve
icing (confectioners') sugar, for dusting

METHOD
Preheat the oven to 160°C (315°F/Gas 2–3). Grease ten
125 ml (4 fl oz/½ cup) ramekins with butter and dust
the inside of each one with caster sugar.

Put the cream and milk in a saucepan over low heat and bring almost to the boil. Add the chocolate and stir over low heat until the chocolate has melted and is well combined. Stir in the orange zest.

Whisk the eggs and extra sugar for 5 minutes, or until pale and thick. Whisk a little of the hot chocolate cream into the eggs, then pour onto the remaining chocolate cream, whisking continuously.

Divide the mixture among the ramekins. Place the ramekins in a roasting tin. Pour enough boiling water into the tin to come halfway up the sides of the ramekins. Cover with foil and bake for 30–35 minutes, or until the custards are set.

Remove the ramekins from the water bath and set aside to cool completely. Turn the custards out onto serving plates. Top with raspberries and dust with icing sugar before serving.

CHOCOLATE BREAD AND BUTTER PUDDING

PREPARATION 25 MINUTES
COOKING 50 MINUTES
SERVES 4–6

60 g (2¼ oz) unsalted butter
6 slices fruit loaf bread
125 ml (4 fl oz/½ cup) milk
500 ml (17 fl oz/2 cups) cream
115 g (4 oz/½ cup) caster (superfine) sugar
100 g (3⅓ oz) chopped dark chocolate
4 eggs, at room temperature, lightly beaten
90 g (3¼ oz/½ cup) dark choc bits
2 tablespoons golden syrup

METHOD
Preheat the oven to 160°C (315°F/Gas 2–3).
Brush a 1 litre (35 fl oz/4 cup) baking dish with oil
or melted butter.

Spread butter on the slices of bread and cut into
diagonal quarters. Place in the dish in a single layer,
overlapping the quarters.

Combine the milk, cream and sugar in a saucepan and stir over low heat until the sugar dissolves. Bring to the boil and remove from the heat. Add the chocolate and stir until melted and smooth. Cool slightly, then gradually whisk in the eggs.

Pour half of the custard over the bread. Stand 10 minutes, or until the bread absorbs most of the liquid. Pour over the remaining custard. Sprinkle with the chocolate bits and drizzle with golden syrup. Bake for 40–45 minutes, or until set and slightly puffed and golden. Serve warm.

COFFEE LIQUEUR MOCHA SAUCE

PREPARATION 5 MINUTES
COOKING 5 MINUTES
SERVES 6

30 g (1 oz) butter
80 g (2¾ oz/1/2 cup) chopped dark chocolate
170 ml (5½ fl oz/⅔ cup) cream
1 teaspoon instant coffee granules
2 tablespoons coffee-flavoured liqueur (such as Kahlùa)

METHOD

To make the sauce, combine the butter, chocolate,
cream and coffee granules in a saucepan over low heat.
Stir until the chocolate has melted and the mixture is
smooth. Remove from the heat and stir in the liqueur.
Be sure to keep the sauce warm before serving.

PIES, TARTS
AND
PASTRIES

CHOCOLATE FUDGE PECAN PIE

PREPARATION 45 MINUTES
COOKING 1 HOUR 20 MINUTES
SERVES 6

PASTRY
150 g (5½ oz/1¼ cups) plain (all-purpose) flour
2 tablespoons unsweetened cocoa powder
2 tablespoons soft brown sugar
100 g (3½ oz) unsalted butter, chilled and cubed

200 g (7 oz/2 cups) pecan nuts, roughly chopped
100 g (3½ oz/⅔ cup) chopped dark chocolate
95 g (3¼ oz/½ cup) soft brown sugar
170 ml (5½ fl oz/⅔ cup) light or dark corn syrup
3 eggs, at room temperature, lightly beaten
2 teaspoons vanilla extract

METHOD
Preheat the oven to 180°C (350°F/Gas 4). Grease a
23 x 18 x 3 cm (9 x 7 x 1¼ inch) pie dish.

To make the pastry, sift the flour, cocoa and sugar into
a bowl and rub in the butter with your fingertips until
the mixture resembles fine breadcrumbs. Make a well
and add 2–3 tablespoons iced water and mix with a
knife, adding more water if necessary.

Lift the dough onto a sheet of baking paper. Press into a disc, cover with plastic wrap and refrigerate for 20 minutes. Roll out the dough between two sheets of baking paper to fit the dish. Line the dish with the dough and trim the edges. Refrigerate for 20 minutes.

Cover the pastry with crumpled baking paper and fill with baking beads or rice. Bake for 15 minutes, remove paper and beads and bake for 15–20 minutes, or until the base is dry. Cool completely.

Place the pie dish on a flat baking tray to catch any drips. Spread the pecans and chocolate over the pastry base. Whisk the sugar, corn syrup, eggs and vanilla in a jug. Pour into the pastry shell and bake for 45 minutes (the filling will still be a bit wobbly, but will set on cooling). Cool before cutting to serve.

BANANA CREAM PIE

PREPARATION 20 MINUTES
COOKING 25 MINUTES
SERVES 6–8

375 g (13 oz) shortcrust pastry
80 g (2¾ oz/½ cup) dark chocolate chips
4 egg yolks, at room temperature
115 g (4 oz/½ cup) caster (superfine) sugar
½ teaspoon vanilla extract
2 tablespoons custard powder
500 ml (17 fl oz/2 cups) milk
40 g (1½ oz) unsalted butter, softened
1 teaspoon brandy or rum
3 large ripe bananas, cut into 3–4 mm (¼ inch) slices
sliced banana, extra, to decorate
1 tablespoon grated dark chocolate, to decorate

METHOD
Roll out the pastry between two sheets of
baking paper to line the base of a 23 x 18 x 3 cm
(9 x 7 x 1¼ inch) baking dish. Remove the top sheet
of paper and invert the pastry into the tin. Trim
the excess and refrigerate for 20 minutes.

Preheat the oven to 190°C (375°F/Gas 5). Line the pastry with crumpled baking paper and cover with baking beads or rice. Bake for 10 minutes, remove the paper and beads, then bake for 10 minutes, or until the pastry is dry and cooked through. While still hot, cover with the chocolate chips. Leave for 5 minutes to soften, then spread the melted chocolate over the base.

Beat the egg yolks, sugar, vanilla and custard powder with electric beaters for 2–3 minutes, or until thick. Bring the milk to the boil in a saucepan over medium heat, remove from the heat and gradually pour into the egg mixture, stirring well. Return the custard filling to the saucepan and bring to the boil, stirring well for 2 minutes, or until thick. Remove from the heat, stir in the butter and brandy, stirring until the butter has melted, then leave to cool.

Arrange the banana slices over the chocolate, then pour over the custard. Decorate with the extra banana and grated chocolate.

SICILIAN CANNOLI

PREPARATION 40 MINUTES
COOKING 10 MINUTES
MAKES 18

PASTRY

250 g (9 oz/2 cups) plain (all-purpose) flour
2 teaspoons instant coffee granules
2 teaspoons unsweetened cocoa powder
2 tablespoons caster (superfine) sugar
60 g (2¼ oz) unsalted butter, chilled and chopped

FILLING

250 g (9 oz) ricotta cheese
185 g (6½ oz/1½ cups) icing (confectioners') sugar
1 teaspoon orange flower water
30 g (1 oz/¼ cup) grated dark chocolate
60 g (2¼ oz) candied citrus peel
icing (confectioners') sugar, to dust

METHOD

To make the pastry, combine the flour, coffee, cocoa, sugar and a pinch of salt. Rub the butter into the flour to make fine breadcrumbs, then work in up to 125 ml (4 fl oz/½ cup) water to make a soft dough. Knead lightly and divide in two. Roll each half out between two sheets of baking paper until about 3 mm (⅛ inch) thick. Cut into 7.5 cm (2¾ inch) squares (18 in total). Place metal cannoli moulds or cannelloni pasta tubes diagonally across the squares and fold the corners across to overlap in the middle. Moisten the overlapping dough, then press firmly to seal. (If you use cannelloni pasta tubes, discard them after frying.)

In a saucepan, deep-fry the tubes, a few at a time, in hot oil deep enough to cover them. When golden and crisp, remove and leave to cool, still on their moulds.

To make the filling, beat the ricotta, icing sugar and orange flower water until smooth. Fold in the chocolate and candied peel. Refrigerate until set.

Slide the pastry tubes off the moulds. Using a piping (icing) bag or a spoon, stuff the tubes with filling, leaving some exposed at each end. Dust with icing sugar before serving.

CHOCOLATE TART

PREPARATION 30 MINUTES
COOKING 30 MINUTES
SERVES 12

375 g (13 oz) shortcrust pastry
50 g (1¾ oz/⅓ cup) chopped dark chocolate
400 g (14 oz/2⅔ cups) chopped milk chocolate
300 ml (10½ fl oz) thick (double/heavy) cream

METHOD
Preheat the oven to 200°C (400°F/Gas 6). Grease
a 35 x 11 cm (14 x 4¼ inch) loose-based tart tin.

Roll out the pastry on a lightly floured work surface
until 3 mm (⅛ inch) thick, to fit the base and sides of
the tin. Roll the pastry onto the rolling pin, then lift
and ease it into the tin, gently pressing to fit into the
corners. Trim the edges, cover with plastic wrap and
refrigerate for 1 hour.

Line the pastry shell with a piece of baking paper and cover the base with baking beads or uncooked rice. Bake the pastry for 10 minutes, then remove the paper and beads and bake for a further 10 minutes, or until the pastry is golden.

Put the dark chocolate in a heatproof bowl. Half fill a saucepan with water, bring to the boil, then remove from the heat and sit the bowl over the pan (don't let the bowl touch the water or the chocolate will get too hot and seize). Stir occasionally until the chocolate melts. Brush the base of the pastry with the melted chocolate.

Put the milk chocolate and cream in a small heatproof bowl. Sit the bowl over a small saucepan of simmering water, stirring until the chocolate has melted and the mixture is smooth. Allow the chocolate to cool slightly, then pour into the pastry case. Refrigerate overnight, or until the chocolate filling has set. Serve the tart in small slices as it is very rich.

CHOCOLATE RICOTTA TART

PREPARATION 20 MINUTES
COOKING 1 HOUR
SERVES 8–10

185 g (6½ oz/1½ cups) plain (all-purpose) flour
100 g (3½ oz) unsalted butter, chopped
2 tablespoons caster (superfine) sugar

FILLING
1.25 kg (2 lb 12 oz) ricotta cheese
125 g (4 oz/½ cup) caster (superfine) sugar
2 tablespoons plain (all-purpose) flour
1 teaspoon instant coffee granules
125 g (4½ oz) finely chopped chocolate
4 egg yolks, at room temperature
40 g (1¼ oz) chocolate, extra
½ teaspoon vegetable oil

METHOD
To make the pastry, sift the flour into a large bowl and
add the butter. Rub the butter into the flour with your
fingertips, until fine and crumbly. Stir in the sugar.
Add 60 ml (2 fl oz/¼ cup) cold water and cut with
a knife to form a dough, adding a little more water if
necessary. Turn out onto a lightly floured surface
and gather into a ball.

Lightly grease a 25 cm (10 inch) spring-form cake tin. Roll out the dough, then line the tin so that the pastry comes about two-thirds of the way up the side. Cover with plastic wrap and refrigerate while making the filling. Preheat the oven to 180°C (350°F/Gas 4).

To make the filling, combine the ricotta, sugar, flour and a pinch of salt until smooth. Dissolve the coffee in 2 teaspoons hot water. Stir into the ricotta mixture, with the chocolate and egg yolks, until well mixed. Spoon into the chilled pastry shell and smooth the surface. Chill for 30 minutes, or until firm.

Put the cake tin on a baking tray. Bake for 1 hour, or until firm. Turn off the oven and leave the tart in the oven to cool with the door ajar (the tart may crack slightly but this will not be noticeable when it cools and has been decorated).

To decorate, melt the extra chocolate and stir in the oil. With a fork, flick thin drizzles of melted chocolate over the tart, or pipe over for a neater finish. Cool completely before cutting into wedges for serving.

THREE CHOCOLATES TART

PREPARATION 30 MINUTES
COOKING 35 MINUTES
SERVES 8

PASTRY
150 g (5½ oz/1¼ cups) plain (all-purpose) flour
20 g (¾ oz) unsweetened cocoa powder
75 g (2½ oz) unsalted butter, chilled and cubed
3 tablespoons caster (superfine) sugar
4 egg yolks, at room temperature
¼ teaspoon vanilla extract

FILLING
110 g (3¾ oz/¾ cup) chopped white chocolate
3 tablespoons liquid glucose
200 g (7 oz/1⅓ cups) chopped dark chocolate
300 ml (10½ fl oz) cream, for whipping

GANACHE
30 g (1 oz/¼ cup) chopped dark chocolate
15 g (½ oz) unsalted butter
1 tablespoon cream

METHOD
To make the pastry, process the flour, cocoa and
unsalted butter in a food processor to form fine
breadcrumbs. Add the sugar using the pulse action,
then add the egg yolks, vanilla and 1 tablespoon water.

Process to form a smooth dough. Flatten to a disc, cover with plastic wrap and chill for 45 minutes. Preheat oven to 180°C (350°F/Gas 4). Grease a 20 cm (8 inch) loose-based tart tin. Roll pastry out thinly between two sheets of baking paper and use to line the tin, pressing it into the flutes. Cover with a sheet of baking paper, fill with baking beads or rice and bake for 12 minutes. Remove the paper and beads and bake for 5 minutes more, or until crisp and dry. Cool completely. To make the filling, put the white chocolate in a bowl set over a pan of simmering water (don't let the bowl touch the water or the chocolate will get too hot and seize). Heat until melted and smooth. Spoon into the tart case and spread evenly over the base. Cool until set.

Put the glucose and dark chocolate in a heatproof bowl set over a saucepan of simmering water. Heat, stirring often, until melted. It will be very thick and tacky. Allow to cool. Whip the cream until stiff peaks form. Fold a heaped spoonful of cream into the chocolate mixture to loosen it. Add the rest of the cream and fold through; the mixture will become very smooth and glossy. Spoon into the tart case, leaving it in broad swirls across the surface. Refrigerate until set.

To make the ganache, put the chocolate, butter and cream in a bowl set over a saucepan of simmering water. Stir until smooth and glossy. Remove from the heat and cool. Spoon ganache into a piping (icing) bag and pipe a criss-cross pattern over the tart. Refrigerate before serving to set.

CHOCOLATE ORANGE TARTS

PREPARATION 45 MINUTES
COOKING 50 MINUTES
SERVES 6

90 g (3¼ oz/¾ cup) plain (all-purpose) flour, sifted
50 g (1¾ oz/¼ cup) rice flour
55 g (2 oz/½ cup) ground almonds
1 tablespoon sugar
125 g (4½ oz) unsalted butter, chopped
1 egg yolk, at room temperature

FILLING
100 g (3½ oz/⅔ cup) chopped dark chocolate
110 g (3¾ oz/¾ cup) chopped milk chocolate
1 teaspoon grated orange zest
2 tablespoons orange juice
310 ml (10¾ fl oz/1¼ cups) cream
2 eggs, at room temperature
3 egg yolks, at room temperature, whisked
whipped cream and candied orange zest, to serve
icing (confectioners') sugar, to dust

METHOD
Preheat oven to 180°C (350°F/Gas 4). Brush
six 12 cm (4 inch) fluted flan tins with melted butter.
In a food processor, process the flours, a pinch of salt,
the ground almonds, sugar and butter for 20 seconds,
or until fine and crumbly. Add the egg yolk and
1–2 tablespoons cold water. Process until the dough
comes together. Divide the dough into six even
portions, then roll out between two sheets of baking
paper to a 6 mm (¼ inch) thickness. Line tart tins with
dough, trim the edges. Refrigerate for 20 minutes.

Cut six sheets of baking paper large enough to cover
the pastry-lined tins. Lay the paper over the pastry and
spread with an even layer of baking beads or rice. Bake
for 15 minutes, then discard the beads and paper and
bake for another 5 minutes.

To make the filling, put the chocolate in a heatproof
bowl. Half fill a saucepan with water, bring to the
boil, then remove from the heat and sit the bowl over
the pan (don't let the bowl touch the water or the
chocolate will get too hot and seize). Stir occasionally
until the chocolate melts, then remove from the heat.

Whisk orange zest, juice, cream, eggs and egg yolks.
Gradually add to the melted chocolate, whisking
constantly. Pour into pastry cases and bake for
20–25 minutes, or until just set (the filling will set
more as tarts cool). Serve warm with whipped cream
and candied orange zest and dust with icing sugar.

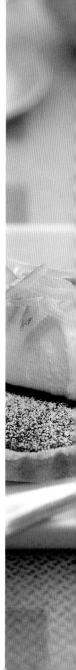

CHOCOLATE HONEYCOMB PASTRIES

PREPARATION 20 MINUTES
COOKING 18 MINUTES
MAKES 18

2 x 24 cm (9½ inch) square sheets ready-rolled
frozen puff pastry
75 g (2 oz/½ cup) finely chopped dark chocolate
50 g (1¾ oz) chopped honeycomb
milk, to brush
icing (confectioners') sugar, to dust

METHOD
Preheat the oven to 220°C (425°F/Gas 7). Line two
baking trays with baking paper.

Lay the puff pastry on a cutting board and cut each
sheet into nine 8 cm (3¼ inch) squares. Set aside for
3–5 minutes, or until thawed slightly.

Meanwhile, combine the chocolate and honeycomb. Divide between the pastry squares, placing the chocolate and honeycomb down the centre on one half.

Fold the pastry squares in half to enclose the filling and then press the edges firmly with a fork to seal. Place the pastries on the baking trays about 3 cm (1¼ inch) apart and brush with a little milk.

Bake for 15–18 minutes, or until golden and puffed. Cool slightly before serving, sprinkled with icing sugar.

CARAMEL TARTS WITH CHOCOLATE GANACHE

PREPARATION 25 MINUTES
COOKING 25 MINUTES
MAKES 12

GANACHE
100 g (3½ oz/⅔ cup) chopped dark chocolate
2 tablespoons cream

PASTRY
150 g (5½ oz/1¼ cups) plain (all-purpose) flour
90 g (3¼ oz) unsalted butter, chilled and cubed
65 g (¼ oz/heaped ¼ cup) caster (superfine) sugar

FILLING
395 g (13¾ oz) tin sweetened condensed milk
30 g (1 oz) unsalted butter
2 tablespoons golden syrup (light treacle)
1½ tablespoons chopped pistachio nuts, to garnish

METHOD
To make the ganache, melt the chocolate and cream
in a bowl over a saucepan of simmering water, stirring
well until melted. Don't let the bowl touch the water
or the chocolate will get too hot and seize. Remove
from the heat, cool, then refrigerate for 10–15 minutes
until firm but not solid.

Preheat the oven to 180°C (350°F/Gas 4). Grease a 12-hole mini muffin tray. Run a strip of foil across the base and up two sides of each hole, leaving a bit of foil to hang over the sides. These will act as handles to help the removal of the tarts later on.

To make the pastry, put the flour, butter and sugar into a food processor and pulse until the mixture resembles breadcrumbs. Divide among the muffin holes and firmly press the mixture down into the bases with your fingers. Bake for 12–15 minutes, or until lightly golden in colour. While they are still hot, press the bases down with the back of a small teaspoon, as they will have risen a little.

To make the filling, put the condensed milk, butter and golden syrup in a saucepan over low heat. Stir until the butter has melted. Increase the heat to medium and simmer for 2–3 minutes, stirring constantly, until light caramel in colour. When stirring, ensure that the bottom and side of the pan are scraped to prevent the mixture from catching and scorching.

Divide the caramel among the pastry bases and cool for 5 minutes. Gently remove the tarts from the tin, then transfer to a wire rack to cool completely.

To serve, whisk the ganache well. Put into a piping (icing) bag with a medium-sized star nozzle and pipe swirls on top of the caramel. Sprinkle with the pistachios. Store in the refrigerator, covered, until set. Remove 10–15 minutes before serving.

CHOCOLATE MOUSSE FLAN

PREPARATION 35 MINUTES
COOKING 5 MINUTES
SERVES 8–10

200 g (7 oz/1½ cups) chocolate cookie crumbs
100 g (3½ oz) unsalted butter, melted

CHOCOLATE CREAM
100 g (3½ oz/⅔ cup) chopped dark chocolate
50 ml (1¾ fl oz/¼ cup) cream

MOCHA MOUSSE
200 g (7 oz) dark chocolate, melted
60 g (2¼ oz) unsalted butter, melted
50 ml (1¾ fl oz/¼) cup thick (double/heavy) cream
2 egg yolks, at room temperature
2 teaspoons instant coffee powder
2 teaspoons powdered gelatine
unsweetened cocoa powder, to dust

METHOD

Brush a 23 cm (9 inch) round, loose-based, fluted flan tin with melted butter or oil.

Combine the cookie crumbs and butter. Press into the base and side of the tin. Refrigerate for 20 minutes, or until firm.

To make the chocolate cream, place the chocolate and cream in a heatproof bowl and set the bowl over a pan of simmering water until the chocolate melts and is smooth. Spread evenly over the flan base. Refrigerate until set.

To make the mocha mousse, combine the chocolate, butter, cream and egg yolks. Meanwhile, combine the coffee and 1 teaspoon boiling water then add to the mixture.

Sprinkle the gelatine over 1 tablespoon water in a small bowl. Stand the bowl in a pan of hot water and stir until the gelatine dissolves. Add the gelatine to the chocolate and stir until smooth.

Using electric beaters, beat the cream until soft peaks form, then fold into the chocolate. Spread over the flan and refrigerate until set.

Cut a star-shaped stencil from stiff cardboard. Place over the flan and dust with cocoa powder. Carefully lift off the stencil. Slice the flan into wedges and serve.

DRIED FRUIT AND CHOCOLATE PILLOWS

PREPARATION 20 MINUTES
COOKING 15 MINUTES
MAKES 24

CREAM CHEESE PASTRY
90 g (3¼ oz/⅓ cup) cream cheese, softened
55 g (2¼ oz/¼ cup) caster (superfine) sugar
1 egg yolk, at room temperature
60 ml (2 fl oz/¼ cup) milk
185 g (6½ oz/1½ cups) plain (all-purpose) flour
1 teaspoon baking powder
1 egg white, at room temperature, to glaze

DRIED FRUIT FILLING
60 g (2¼ oz/⅓ cup) chopped dried figs
95 g (3¼ oz/½ cup) chopped dried apricots
60 g (2¼ oz/½ cup) raisins, chopped
60 g (2¼ oz) chopped dark chocolate
½ teaspoon grated lemon zest
80 g (2¾ oz/¼ cup) clear honey
large pinch ground allspice
large pinch ground cinnamon

METHOD

To make the cream cheese pastry, beat the cheese and sugar until fluffy. Beat in the egg yolk and milk, then sift in the flour, a pinch of salt and the baking powder and form into a smooth dough. Cover with plastic wrap and refrigerate for 2 hours.

To make the dried fruit filling, put all the ingredients in a food processor and pulse until finely chopped.

Preheat the oven to 180°C (350°F/Gas 4). Divide the fruit filling into three equal portions and roll each portion into a 32 cm (12½ inch) long rope. Divide the pastry into three and, on a lightly floured surface, roll out to 10 x 32 cm (4 x 12½ inch) rectangles.

Brush one length of a rectangle with water. Lay a portion of filling on the strip of pastry near the dry side. Roll the pastry over and press to seal, then cut into eight diagonal pieces and lay, seam side down, on an ungreased baking tray. Repeat with the remaining pastry and filling.

Mix the egg white with 1 tablespoon cold water and glaze the pillows. Bake for 13–15 minutes, or until golden. Leave to cool on the tray for 2–3 minutes, then transfer to a wire rack.

COCOA-SCENTED TEA

PREPARATION 10 MINUTES
COOKING NIL
MAKES 12 CUPS OF TEA

50 g (1¾ oz/⅓ cup) Callebaut cocoa nibs (100% roasted
cocoa nibs)
2 tablespoons English Breakfast tea leaves
2 vanilla beans, finely chopped

METHOD
Combine the cocoa nibs, tea leaves and vanilla beans
in a glass jar. Seal and store for at least 2 weeks to
infuse before using.

Place 2 teaspoons of cocoa-scented tea in a tea ball.
Place the tea ball in a 250 ml (9 fl oz/1 cup) heatproof
glass. Add 185 ml (6 fl oz/¾ cup) of just boiling water
and set aside to infuse for 5 minutes. Remove the tea
ball. Add 1 teaspoon of sugar (or to taste) and milk,
if desired. Serve immediately.

CHILLED DESSERTS AND SWEETS

LEMON COCONUT TRUFFLES

PREPARATION 10 MINUTES
COOKING 5 MINUTES
MAKES 40

60 ml (2 fl oz/¼ cup) cream
250 g (9 oz/1⅔ cups) white chocolate melts
1 tablespoon grated lemon zest
2 teaspoons lemon juice
45 g (1½ oz/½ cup) desiccated coconut
40 g (1½ oz/¾ cup) shredded coconut, toasted

METHOD
Heat the cream and chocolate in a saucepan over
low heat until the chocolate just melts. Remove from
the heat and stir in the lemon zest, lemon juice and
desiccated coconut. Leave to cool for 30 minutes,
then refrigerate for 1½ hours.

Roll the mixture into balls and place on a foil-lined
tray and refrigerate for 45 minutes. Once set, roll the
balls in the shredded coconut.

CHOCOLATE AND AMARETTI REFRIGERATOR CAKE

PREPARATION 30 MINUTES
COOKING 5 MINUTES
SERVES 8

250 g (9 oz/1⅔ cups) chopped dark chocolate
1 tablespoon instant coffee granules
250 g (9 oz) unsalted butter, softened
185 g (6½ oz/1 cup) raw caster (superfine) sugar
1 tablespoon unsweetened cocoa powder
3 eggs, at room temperature, separated
50 g (1¾ oz/½ cup) flaked almonds, toasted
50 g (1¾ oz/¼ cup) glacé (candied) cherries, halved
300 g (10½ oz) amaretti biscuits
2 tablespoons cognac

METHOD

Line a 22 cm (8½ inch) spring-form cake tin
with plastic wrap. Put the chocolate in a heatproof
bowl. Half fill a saucepan with water and bring to the
boil. Sit the bowl over the pan, but don't let the bowl
touch the water or the chocolate will get too hot and
seize. Stir frequently until the chocolate has melted,
slowly adding in the coffee, then leave to cool.

Beat the butter and sugar with electric beaters until light and fluffy, then sift in the cocoa and beat well. Add the egg yolks one at a time, beating well after each addition. Fold in the melted chocolate.

In a separate bowl, whisk the egg whites until stiff peaks form. Using a metal spoon, gently fold into the chocolate mixture. Add the almonds and glacé cherries and fold through.

Put a tightly fitting single layer of amaretti on the base of the tin, flat side down. Drizzle a little cognac over them. Spread half the chocolate on top, then cover with another layer of amaretti. Drizzle with cognac, cover with the rest of the chocolate mixture and put a final tight layer of amaretti on top, flat side down. Knock the tin on the work surface a couple of times to pack the cake layers down. Cover the top with plastic wrap and refrigerate overnight.

Remove the cake from the tin. It will be sufficiently set to enable you to upturn it onto one hand, peel off the plastic wrap and set it down on a serving plate, right way up. Cut into wedges to serve.

WHITE CHOCOLATE AND COCONUT SEMIFREDDO WITH BLACKBERRIES

PREPARATION 30 MINUTES
COOKING 20 MINUTES
SERVES 8

170 ml (5½ fl oz/⅔ cup) milk
45 g (1¾ oz/½ cup) desiccated coconut
100 g (3½ oz/⅔ cup) chopped white chocolate
2 egg yolks, at room temperature
55 g (2 oz/¼ cup) caster (superfine) sugar
185 ml (6 fl oz/¾ cup) cream, lightly whipped

BLACKBERRIES IN SYRUP
2 tablespoons caster (superfine) sugar
300 g (10½ oz) blackberries

METHOD
Spray a 750 ml (26 fl oz/3 cup) bar (loaf) tin with oil,
then line it with plastic wrap (the oil will help you
get the creases out of the wrap, so your semifreddo
will have a smoother finish). Leave the wrap to hang
over the sides of the tin.

Put the milk and coconut in a saucepan over medium heat and bring to a simmer. Remove from the heat, cover and cool to room temperature. Strain through a fine sieve, pressing with the back of a spoon to extract as much milk as possible. There should be about 80 ml (2½ fl oz/⅓ cup).

Put the chocolate in a saucepan over low heat, stir in the infused milk, stirring until the chocolate melts. Remove from the heat.

Whisk the egg yolks and sugar in a heatproof bowl over a pan of simmering water until very thick and pale. Stir in the chocolate mixture. Fold in the whipped cream in two batches. Pour into the tin and smooth the surface. Cover with the overhanging plastic wrap and freeze for 6 hours, or until frozen.

Just before serving prepare the blackberries. Put the sugar in a small pan with 2 tablespoons of water and stir over low heat until the sugar has dissolved. Bring to a simmer, add the blackberries and briefly warm through.

Tip out the semifreddo onto a chopping board and peel away the plastic wrap. Cut into slices and serve with the blackberries and syrup.

MOCHA COFFEE CREAM POTS

PREPARATION 40 MINUTES
COOKING 35 MINUTES
SERVES 6

600 ml (21 fl oz) cream
50 g (1¾ oz/⅔ cup) roasted coffee beans
100 g (3½ oz/⅔ cup) chopped dark chocolate
6 egg yolks, at room temperature
55 g (2 oz/¼ cup) caster (superfine) sugar
3 teaspoons Tia Maria or other coffee liqueur
whipped cream and chocolate-coated coffee beans

METHOD

Preheat the oven to 150°C (300°F/Gas 2). Put the cream, coffee beans and chocolate into a saucepan. Stir over low heat until the chocolate melts, then bring to a simmer and cook for 2–3 minutes. Remove from the heat. Leave for 30 minutes to allow the coffee to infuse.

Whisk the egg yolks, sugar and liqueur. Strain in the coffee-infused milk, stir, then divide among six 125 ml (4 fl oz/½ cup) ramekins. Put in a roasting tin and pour enough boiling water into the tin to come halfway up the sides of the ramekins. Bake for 25–30 minutes. Remove from the oven and leave to cool. Refrigerate overnight or until set. Serve with whipped cream and coffee beans.

FRECKLES

PREPARATION 10 MINUTES
COOKING 5 MINUTES
MAKES 12

150 g (5½ oz/1 cup) milk chocolate melts
sprinkles of your choice (such as 100s and 1000s,
silver or mixed cachous and/or coloured sprinkles)

METHOD
Line a large tray with baking paper.

Put the chocolate in a heatproof bowl. Half fill a
saucepan with water, bring to the boil, then remove
from the heat and sit the bowl over the pan (don't let
the bowl touch the water or the chocolate will get too
hot and seize). Stir occasionally, until the chocolate
just melts. Remove from the heat.

Spoon 2 teaspoon measures of the chocolate onto the
lined tray, spacing them about about 5 cm (2 inches)
apart to form about 12 rounds. Tap the tray on the
bench lightly to spread the chocolate out to form
5 cm (2 inch) discs. Sprinkle the chocolate discs with
sprinkles of your choice. Set aside at room temperature
for 30 minutes, or until set.

PETITS POTS AU CHOCOLAT

PREPARATION 20 MINUTES
COOKING 1 HOUR
SERVES 8

170 ml (5½ fl oz/⅔ cup) thick (double/heavy) cream
½ vanilla bean, split lengthways
150 g (5½ oz/1 cup) chopped dark chocolate
80 ml (2½ fl oz/⅓ cup) milk
2 egg yolks, at room temperature
55 g (2 oz/¼ cup) caster (superfine) sugar
whipped cream, to serve
unsweetened cocoa powder, to serve

METHOD
Lightly brush eight 80 ml (2½ fl oz/⅓ cup) ramekins
with melted butter and put them in a roasting tin.
Preheat the oven to 140°C (275°F/Gas 1). Heat the
cream in a small pan with the vanilla bean until the
cream is warm. Leave to infuse for 10 minutes then
scrape the seeds out of the vanilla bean into the cream,
and discard the empty bean.

Combine the chocolate and milk in a saucepan. Stir constantly over low heat until the chocolate has just melted.

Place the egg yolks in a bowl and slowly whisk in the sugar. Continue whisking until the sugar has dissolved and the mixture is light and creamy.

Add the vanilla cream and the melted chocolate to the beaten egg yolks and mix well.

Pour into the ramekins, filling approximately two-thirds of the way up. Pour enough boiling water into the roasting tin to come halfway up the sides of the ramekins. Bake for 45 minutes, or until the chocolate pots have puffed up slightly and feel spongy.

Remove from the roasting tin and set aside to cool completely. Cover with plastic wrap and refrigerate for 6 hours before serving. Serve with a dollop of cream and a sprinkle of sifted cocoa.

CHOCOLATE PANNA COTTA WITH POACHED RAISINS

PREPARATION 20 MINUTES
COOKING 10 MINUTES
SERVES 6

300 ml (10½ fl oz) cream
185 ml (6 fl oz/¾ cup) milk
2 tablespoons caster (superfine) sugar
150 g (5½ oz) finely chopped milk chocolate
2 teaspoons powdered gelatine

POACHED RAISINS
125 g (4½ oz/1 cup) raisins
60 ml (2 fl oz/¼ cup) Pedro Ximenez,
or other sweet sherry

METHOD
Combine the cream, milk and sugar in a small
saucepan. Stir over medium heat until the sugar
dissolves. Bring to a simmer, then remove from the
heat and add the chocolate. Stir until the chocolate
melts and is well combined.

Place 2 teaspoons boiling water in a heatproof bowl.
Sprinkle the gelatine over and use a fork to stir until
the gelatine dissolves. Set aside for 1 minute, or until
the liquid is clear. Add to the hot chocolate mixture
and mix well. Strain into a jug. Cover and place in
the fridge, stirring occasionally, for 1 hour or until
cooled to room temperature.

Very lightly brush six 125 ml (4 fl oz/½ cup) ramekins
with canola oil, to grease. Place on a tray. Stir the
cooled chocolate mixture and then divide it evenly
among the ramekins. Place in the fridge for 6 hours,
or until lightly set.

To make the poached raisins, combine the raisins and
2 tablespoons water in a small saucepan. Over low
heat, gently simmer for 5 minutes, or until the raisins
are soft and a light syrup has formed.

To serve, slide a palette knife down the side of
each mould, one at a time, to create an air pocket,
then turn out onto serving plates. Serve accompanied
with the poached raisins.

CHOCOLATE BAVAROIS

PREPARATION 30 MINUTES
COOKING 10 MINUTES
SERVES 6

250 g (7 oz/1⅔ cups) chopped dark chocolate
375 ml (13 fl oz/1½ cups) milk
4 egg yolks, at room temperature
80 g (2¾ oz/⅓ cup) caster (superfine) sugar
1 tablespoon powdered gelatine
315 ml (10⅓ fl oz/1¼ cups) cream, for whipping
chocolate flakes, to serve

METHOD
Combine the chocolate and milk in a small saucepan.
Stir over a low heat until the chocolate has melted and
the milk just comes to the boil. Remove from the heat.

Beat the egg yolks and sugar until combined, then gradually add the hot chocolate milk, whisking until they are combined. Pour into a cleaned saucepan and over low heat, gently stir until the mixture is thick enough to coat the back of a wooden spoon. Do not allow it to boil. Remove from the heat.

Put 2 tablespoons water in a small heatproof bowl, sprinkle the gelatine in an even layer over the surface and leave to go spongy. Stir into the hot chocolate mixture until it dissolves. Refrigerate until cold but not set, stirring occasionally.

Beat the cream until soft peaks form, then fold into the chocolate mixture in two batches. Pour into six parfait glasses and refrigerate for several hours or overnight, or until set. Serve cold, topped with chocolate flakes.

CHOCOLATE CREME CARAMEL

PREPARATION 25 MINUTES
COOKING 55 MINUTES
MAKES 4

185 g (6 oz/¾ cup) caster (superfine) sugar

CUSTARD
4 egg yolks, at room temperature
60 g (2 oz/¼ cup) caster (superfine) sugar
315 ml (10¾ fl oz/1¼ cups) milk
185 ml (6 fl oz/¾ cup) cream
150 g (5½ oz/1 cup) chopped dark chocolate
whipped cream, to serve

METHOD
Preheat oven to 160°C (315°F/ Gas 2–3).
Combine the sugar and 185 ml (6 fl oz/¾ cup) water
in a small saucepan. Stir over low heat without boiling
until the sugar has dissolved. Bring to the boil and
then reduce the heat. Simmer until the syrup just turns
golden. Quickly pour the caramel into four
250 ml (9 fl oz/1 cup) ramekins. Allow to set.

To make the custard, whisk the egg yolks and sugar until just combined and slightly thickened. Combine the milk and cream in a saucepan.

Bring to the boil, then remove from the heat. Add the chocolate to the milk and stir until melted. Gradually whisk into the egg mixture. Pour the custard through a fine strainer into a large jug. Pour the chocolate custard into the caramel-lined ramekins.

Place the ramekins in a roasting tin. Pour enough boiling water into the tin to come halfway up the sides of the ramekins. Bake for 45 minutes, or until the custard is just set (the custard will set more on standing). Remove from the water bath and set aside until cooled. Refrigerate overnight. Run a knife around the inside edge of each ramekin before turning out onto serving plates. Serve plain or with whipped cream and broken toffee pieces.

COFFEE CREMETS WITH CHOCOLATE SAUCE

PREPARATION 20 MINUTES
COOKING 5 MINUTES
SERVES 4

250 g (9 oz/1 cup) cream cheese, softened
250 ml (9 fl oz/1 cup) thick (double/heavy) cream
80 ml (2½ oz/⅓ cup) very strong coffee
80 g (2¾ oz/⅓ cup) caster (superfine) sugar

CHOCOLATE SAUCE
100 g (3½ oz) dark chocolate
50 g (1¾ oz) unsalted butter

METHOD
Line four 100 ml (3½ fl oz) ramekins with muslin
(cheesecloth), leaving enough muslin hanging over
the side to wrap over the crémet.

Beat the cream cheese until smooth, then whisk in the cream. Add the coffee and sugar and mix well. Spoon into the ramekins and fold the muslin over the top.

Refrigerate for at least 1½ hours, then unwrap the muslin and turn the crémets out onto individual plates, carefully peeling the muslin off each one.

To make the chocolate sauce, gently melt the chocolate in a saucepan with the butter and 80 ml (2½ oz/⅓ cup) water. Stir well to make a shiny sauce, then allow the sauce to cool. Pour a little chocolate sauce over each crémet.

CHEWY CARAMEL AND WALNUT LOGS

PREPARATION 20 MINUTES
COOKING 20 MINUTES
MAKES 70

125 g (4½ oz) butter, cubed
395 g (14 oz) tin sweetened condensed milk
2 tablespoons golden syrup or light treacle
160 g (5½ oz/¾ cup firmly packed) light brown sugar
100 g (3½ oz/¾ cup) finely chopped walnuts, toasted
250 g (9 oz/1⅔ cups) chopped dark chocolate

METHOD
Grease an 18 cm (7 inch) square cake tin and line it
with baking paper, leaving it hanging over the two
opposite sides for easy removal later.

Combine the butter, condensed milk, golden syrup
and sugar in a saucepan over low heat until the butter
melts and the sugar dissolves. Increase the heat a little
so that the mixture bubbles at a steady slow boil. Stir
constantly for about 10 minutes, or until the mixture is
caramel in colour and leaves the side of the pan when
stirred. Stir in the walnuts. Pour into the tin and leave
at room temperature to cool and set.

Remove from the tin, using the baking paper for
handles. Cut into six even pieces. Gently roll each
piece into a log approximately 12 cm (4½ inches) long
and place on a tray lined with baking paper.
Refrigerate for 1 hour, or until firm.

Melt the chocolate in a small bowl over a saucepan of
simmering water. Don't let the bowl touch the water
or the chocolate will get too hot and seize. Coat each
caramel log with the chocolate and return to the tray.
Return to the fridge until set.

About 10 minutes before serving, take as many logs
as you need at the time from the refrigerator. Cut into
slices about 1 cm (½ inch) thick.

CHOCOLATE, GINGER AND NUT PATE

PREPARATION 15 MINUTES
COOKING 5 MINUTES
MAKES 50

250 g (9 oz/1⅔ cups) chopped dark chocolate
20 g (¾ oz) unsalted butter
160 ml (5¼ fl oz) sweetened condensed milk
2 tablespoons rum or brandy
70 g (2½ oz/½ cup) hazelnuts, roasted and skinned
80 g (2¾ oz/½ cup) roasted, unsalted
macadamia nuts
50 g (1¾ oz/⅓ cup) whole almonds, roasted
70 g (2½ oz/⅓ cup) finely chopped glacé
(candied) ginger

METHOD

Grease a 25 x 8 cm (10 x 3¼ inch) loaf (bar) tin and line it with baking paper. Let the paper hang over the long sides for easy removal later.

Put the chocolate in a heatproof bowl. Half fill a saucepan with water, bring to the boil, then remove from the heat and sit the bowl over the pan (don't let the bowl touch the water or the chocolate will get too hot and seize). Stir frequently, until just melted and smooth. Add the butter, condensed milk and rum or brandy. Stir until smooth.

Remove from the heat, add the nuts and ginger and mix well. Spoon into the tin and smooth the surface. Cover and refrigerate for several hours until firm. Serve chilled, cut into wafer-thin slices.

CHUNKY MONKEY PARFAIT

PREPARATION 20 MINUTES
COOKING 10 MINUTES
SERVES 6

CHOCOLATE FUDGE SAUCE
100 g (3½ oz/⅔ cup) chopped dark chocolate
185 ml (6 fl oz/¾ cup) sweetened condensed milk
80 ml (2½ fl oz/⅓ cup) cream
40 g (1½ oz) unsalted butter, diced

MARSHMALLOW FLUFF
90 g (3¼ oz/1 cup) white marshmallows
80 ml (2½ fl oz/⅓ cup) cream

6 scoops chocolate-chip ice cream
6 large pretzels
6 scoops praline ice cream
10 chocolate-coated peanut buttercups, chopped
6 scoops peanut butter ice cream
50 g (1¾ oz/⅓ cup) honey-roasted peanuts

METHOD

To make the chocolate fudge sauce, put the chocolate, condensed milk and cream into a heatproof bowl. Fill a saucepan one-third full with water and bring to a simmer over medium heat. Sit the bowl on top of the saucepan. Stir occasionally until the chocolate has almost melted, then remove from the heat and stir until completely smooth. Beat in the butter until melted and the mixture smooth. Set aside to cool for about 20 minutes, stirring regularly.

To make the marshmallow fluff, finely chop the marshmallows, put them in a saucepan with the cream and melt over low heat until the marshmallows are completely dissolved. Allow to cool, then put in the fridge to chill.

To assemble the sundaes, put a tablespoon of chocolate fudge sauce in each of six tall parfait glasses. Top each with a scoop of chocolate-chip ice cream, some pretzels, a scoop of praline ice cream, some chopped peanut butter cups, then a scoop of the peanut butter ice cream. Press down lightly.

Dollop with the marshmallow fluff. Serve drizzled with extra chocolate fudge sauce and scattered with honey-roasted peanuts.

RUM TRUFFLES

PREPARATION 20 MINUTES
COOKING 2 MINUTES
MAKES 25

200 g (7 oz/1⅓ cups) finely chopped dark chocolate
60 ml (2 fl oz/¼ cup) cream
30 g (1 oz) unsalted butter
50 g (1¾ oz) chocolate cake crumbs
2 teaspoons dark rum
95 g (3¼ oz/½ cup) chocolate sprinkles

METHOD

Line a baking tray with foil. Place the chocolate in
a heatproof bowl. Combine the cream and butter
in a saucepan and stir over low heat until the butter
melts and mixture is just boiling. Pour the hot cream
over the chocolate and stir until the chocolate melts
and the mixture is smooth.

Stir in the cake crumbs and rum. Refrigerate for about
20 minutes, stirring occasionally, or until firm enough
to handle. Roll heaped teaspoons of mixture into balls.

Spread the chocolate sprinkles on a sheet of baking
paper. Roll each truffle in the sprinkles, then place
on the tray. Refrigerate for 30 minutes, or until firm.
Serve in small paper patty cups, if desired.

NO-BAKE CHOCOLATE SQUARES

PREPARATION 15 MINUTES
COOKING 5 MINUTES
MAKES 15

100 g (3½ oz) roughly crushed shortbread
120 g (4¼ oz) pistachio nuts
150 g (5½ oz/1 cup) hazelnuts, roasted and skinned
100 g (3½ oz/½ cup) glacé (candied) cherries,
300 g (10½ oz/2 cups) chopped dark chocolate
200 g (7 oz) unsalted butter, chopped
1 teaspoon instant coffee granules
2 eggs, at room temperature, lightly beaten

METHOD

Lightly grease an 18 x 27 cm (7 x 10¾ inch) baking tin.
Line with baking paper, leaving paper hanging over the
two long sides. Combine crumbs, pistachios, 90 g
(3¼ oz/⅔ cup) of the hazelnuts, and half the cherries.

Heat chocolate and butter in a heatproof bowl over a
pan of simmering water. Stir until melted and smooth.
Remove from heat. Cool, then mix in coffee and eggs.
Pour the chocolate over the crumb and nut mixture
and mix well. Pour into the tin and pat down well.
Roughly chop the rest of the hazelnuts and sprinkle
them over the top, along with the remaining cherries.
Refrigerate overnight. Remove from the tin and trim
the edges before cutting into small pieces.

ROCKY ROAD

PREPARATION 15 MINUTES
COOKING 5 MINUTES
MAKES 30 PIECES

250 g (9 oz/2¾ cups) pink and white
marshmallows, halved
160 g (5½ oz/1 cup) roughly chopped unsalted peanuts
100 g (3½ oz/½ cup) glacé (candied) cherries, halved
60 g (2¼ oz/1 cup) shredded coconut
350 g (12 oz/2⅓ cups) chopped dark chocolate

METHOD
Line the base and two opposite sides of a 20 cm
(8 inch) square cake tin with foil.

Combine the marshmallows, peanuts, cherries and
coconut. Put the chocolate in a heatproof bowl and
set over a saucepan of simmering water. Don't let
the bowl touch the water, or the chocolate will get
too hot and seize. Stir occasionally until just melted
and smooth. Add the chocolate to the marshmallow
mixture and toss together.

Spoon into the tin and press evenly over the base.
Refrigerate for several hours, or until set. Carefully lift
the rocky road out of the tin, then peel away the foil
and cut it into small pieces.

CHOCOLATE CHERRY TRIFLE

PREPARATION 30 MINUTES
COOKING 10 MINUTES
SERVES 6

350 g (12 oz) chocolate cake
2 x 450 g (1 lb) tins pitted dark cherries
60 ml (2 fl oz/¼ cup) Kirsch
2 egg yolks, at room temperature
2 tablespoons sugar
1 tablespoon cornflour (cornstarch)
250 ml (9 fl oz/1 cup) milk
1 teaspoon vanilla extract
185 ml (6 fl oz/¾ cup) cream, whipped
whipped cream, to serve
30 g (1 oz) toasted slivered almonds, to serve

METHOD
Cut the cake into thin strips. Line the base of a
1.75 (6 fl oz/7 cup) litre serving bowl with a third
of the cake. Drain the cherries, reserving the juice.
Combine 250 ml (9 fl oz/1 cup) of the juice with
the Kirsch and sprinkle some liberally over the cake.
Spoon some cherries over the cake.

To make the custard, whisk the egg yolks, sugar and cornflour in a heatproof bowl until thick and pale. Heat the milk in a saucepan and bring almost to the boil. Remove from the heat and add the milk gradually to the egg mixture, beating constantly. Pour the whole mixture back into the pan and stir over medium heat for 5 minutes, or until the custard boils and thickens. Remove from the heat and add the vanilla. Cover the surface with plastic wrap and allow to cool, then fold in the whipped cream.

Spoon a third of the custard over the cherries and cake in the bowl. Top with more cake, syrup, cherries and custard. Continue layering, finishing with custard on top. Cover and refrigerate for 3–4 hours. Top with the extra whipped cream and almonds before serving.

ZUCCOTTO

PREPARATION 1 HOUR
COOKING 10 MINUTES
SERVES 6–8

1 ready-made sponge cake
80 ml (2½ fl oz/⅓ cup) Kirsch
60 ml (2 fl oz/¼ cup) Cointreau
80 ml (2½ fl oz/⅓ cup) rum, cognac,
or Grand Marnier
500 ml (17 fl oz/2 cups) cream, for whipping
90 g (3¼oz) chopped dark roasted almond chocolate
175 g (6 oz) finely chopped mixed glacé (candied) fruit
100 g (3½ oz) dark chocolate, melted
70 g (2½ oz) hazelnuts, roasted and chopped
unsweetened cocoa powder and icing
(confectioners') sugar, to decorate

METHOD
Line a 1.5 litre (52 fl oz/6 cup) pudding basin (mould)
with damp muslin (cheesecloth). Cut the cake into
curved pieces with a knife (you will need about
12 pieces). Work with one strip of cake at a time,
brushing it with the combined liqueurs and arranging
the pieces closely in the basin.

Put the thin ends of the cake in the centre so the slices cover the base and side of the basin. Brush with the remaining liqueur to soak the cake. Put in the fridge to chill.

Beat the cream until stiff peaks form, then divide in half. Fold the almond chocolate and glacé fruit into one half and spread evenly over the cake in the basin, leaving a space in the centre.

Put the chocolate in a heatproof bowl. Half fill a saucepan with water, bring to the boil, then remove from the heat and sit the bowl over the pan (don't let the bowl touch the water or the chocolate will get too hot and seize). Stir occasionally until the chocolate melts. Allow to cool.

Fold the cooled melted chocolate and hazelnuts into the remaining cream and spoon into the centre cavity, packing it in firmly. Smooth the surface, cover and chill for 8 hours to allow the cream to firm slightly. Turn out onto a plate and dust with cocoa powder and icing sugar.

SPECIAL OCCASIONS

BLACK FOREST CAKE

PREPARATION 1 HOUR
COOKING 1 HOUR
SERVES 8–10

185 g (6½ oz) unsalted butter, softened
170 g (6 oz/¾ cup) caster (superfine) sugar
3 eggs, at room temperature, lightly beaten
1 teaspoon vanilla extract
210 g (7½ oz/1⅔ cups) self-raising flour
40 g (1½ oz/⅓ cup) plain (all-purpose) flour
90 g (3 oz/¾ cup) unsweetened cocoa powder
1 tablespoon instant coffee granules
½ teaspoon bicarbonate of soda (baking soda)
125 ml (4 fl oz/½ cup) buttermilk
80 ml (2½ fl oz/⅓ cup) milk
310 ml (10¾ fl oz/1¼ cups) cream, whipped
425 g (15 oz) tin pitted cherries, drained
chocolate curls, for decoration

CHOCOLATE TOPPING
300 g (10½ oz/2 cups) chopped dark chocolate
375 g (13 oz) unsalted butter, softened

METHOD
Preheat the oven to 180°C (350°F/Gas 4). Grease a
23 cm (9 inch) round cake tin and line the base and
side with baking paper.

Cream the butter and sugar with electric beaters until light and fluffy. Add the eggs gradually, beating thoroughly after each addition. Add the vanilla and beat until well combined.

Using a metal spoon, fold in the sifted flours, cocoa, coffee and bicarbonate of soda alternately with the combined buttermilk and milk. Stir until almost smooth.

Pour into the tin and smooth the surface. Bake for 40–50 minutes, or until a skewer comes out clean when poked into the centre of the cake. Leave in the tin for 20 minutes before turning out onto a wire rack to cool.

To make the chocolate topping, put the chocolate in a heatproof bowl. Half fill a saucepan with water and bring to the boil. Sit the bowl over the pan, but don't let the bowl touch the water or the chocolate will get too hot and seize. Allow to stand, stirring occasionally, until the chocolate has melted. Beat the butter until light and creamy. Add the chocolate, beating for 1 minute, or until the mixture is glossy and smooth.

Turn the cake upside down and cut into three layers horizontally. Place the first layer on a serving plate. Spread evenly with half the whipped cream, then top with half the cherries. Continue layering with the remaining cake, cream and cherries, ending with the cake on the top, cut side down. Spread the chocolate topping over the top and side. Using a piping (icing) bag and the remaining topping, pipe swirls around the cake rim. Decorate with chocolate curls.

ANGEL FOOD CAKE WITH CHOCOLATE SAUCE

PREPARATION 30 MINUTES
COOKING 50 MINUTES
SERVES 8

125 g (4½ oz/1 cup) plain (all-purpose) flour
230 g (8 oz/1 cup) caster (superfine) sugar
10 egg whites, at room temperature
1 teaspoon cream of tartar
½ teaspoon vanilla extract

CHOCOLATE SAUCE
250 g (9 oz/1⅔ cups) chopped dark chocolate
185 ml (6 fl oz/¾ cup) cream
50 g (1¾ oz) chopped unsalted butter

METHOD
Preheat the oven to 180°C (350°F/Gas 4). Have an
ungreased angel cake tin ready. Sift the flour and half
the sugar four times into a large bowl. Set aside.

Beat the egg whites, cream of tartar and ¼ teaspoon salt with electric beaters until soft peaks form. Gradually add the remaining sugar and beat until thick and glossy. Add the vanilla.

Sift half the flour and sugar mixture over the meringue and gently fold in with a metal spoon. Do the same with the rest of the flour and sugar. Spoon into the tin and bake for 45 minutes, or until a skewer comes out clean when poked into the centre of the cake. Gently loosen around the side of the cake with a spatula, then turn the cake out onto a wire rack to cool completely.

To make the chocolate sauce, put the chocolate, cream and butter in a saucepan. Stir over low heat until the chocolate has melted and the mixture is smooth. Drizzle over the cake and serve.

YULE LOG

60 g (2¼ oz/½ cup) plain (all-purpose) flour
2 tablespoons unsweetened cocoa powder
3 eggs, at room temperature
80 g (2¾ oz/⅓ cup) caster (superfine) sugar,
plus extra to sprinkle
50 g (1¾ oz) unsalted butter, melted and cooled

FILLING
125 g (4½ oz) white chocolate, chopped
125 ml (4 fl oz/½ cup) cream
50 g (1¾ oz) finely chopped toasted hazelnuts

TOPPING
125 g (4½ oz) chopped dark chocolate
125 ml (4 fl oz/½ cup) cream
icing (confectioners') sugar, to dust

METHOD
Preheat the oven to 180°C (350°F/Gas 4). Brush a
30 x 35 cm (12 x 14 inch) Swiss roll tin (jelly roll tin)
with oil or melted butter and line the base and sides
with baking paper. Sift the flour and cocoa together
twice. Using electric beaters, beat the eggs and sugar
for 5 minutes, or until light, fluffy and thick.

Sift the flour and cocoa mixture over the eggs and pour the butter around the edge of the bowl. Using a metal spoon, gently fold in the flour and butter.

Spread into the tin and bake for 12 minutes, or until a skewer comes out clean when poked into the centre of the cake. Sprinkle the extra caster sugar over a clean tea towel (dish towel). Turn the sponge out onto the tea towel close to one end. Roll up the sponge and tea towel together lengthways and leave to cool.

To make the filling, put the white chocolate in a small heatproof bowl. Bring a saucepan of water to the boil, then remove from the heat. Add the cream to the chocolate and sit the bowl over the pan of water, making sure the bowl does not touch the water, until the chocolate is soft. Stir until smooth. Do this for the dark chocolate and cream for the topping. Leave the white chocolate mixture until it has cooled and is the consistency of cream. Leave the dark chocolate mixture until it cools and is spreadable.

Beat the white chocolate mixture with electric beaters just until soft peaks form. Unroll the sponge, remove the tea towel and spread the sponge with the filling, finishing 2 cm (¾ inch) from the end. Sprinkle with hazelnuts, reroll and trim the ends. Cut off one end on the diagonal and place it alongside the log to create a branch. Spread dark chocolate topping all over the log. Run a fork along the length of the roll to give a 'bark' effect. Just before serving, decorate with fresh unsprayed green leaves and dust with icing sugar.

CHOCOLATE ECLAIRS

PREPARATION 20 MINUTES
COOKING 40 MINUTES
MAKES 18

125 g (4½ oz) unsalted butter
125 g (4½ oz/1 cup) plain (all-purpose) flour, sifted
4 eggs, at room temperature, lightly beaten
300 ml (10 fl oz) cream, whipped
150 g (5½ oz/1 cup) chopped dark chocolate

METHOD
Preheat the oven to 210°C (415°F/Gas 6–7). Grease
two baking trays. Combine the butter and 250 ml
(9 fl oz/1 cup) water in a saucepan. Stir over medium
heat until the butter melts. Increase the heat, bring
to the boil, then remove from the heat.

Add the flour to the saucepan and quickly beat into butter mixture with a wooden spoon. Return to the heat and continue beating until the mixture leaves the side of the pan and forms a ball. Transfer to a large bowl and cool slightly. Beat the mixture to release any remaining heat. Gradually add the egg, 3 teaspoons at a time. Beat well after each addition until all the egg has been added and the mixture is glossy (a wooden spoon should stand upright). It will be too runny if the egg is added too quickly. If this happens, beat for several more minutes, or until thickened.

Spoon into a piping (icing) bag fitted with a 1.5 cm (½ inch) plain nozzle. Sprinkle the baking trays lightly with water. Pipe 15 cm (6 inch) lengths onto the trays, leaving room for expansion. Bake for 10–15 minutes. Reduce heat to 180°C (350°F/Gas 4) and bake for another 15 minutes, or until golden and firm. Cool on a wire rack. Split each éclair, and remove any uncooked dough. Fill the éclairs with cream.

Put the chocolate in a heatproof bowl. Half fill a saucepan with water, bring to the boil, then remove the pan from the heat. Sit the bowl over the pan, making sure the bowl doesn't touch the water or the chocolate will get too hot and seize. Allow to stand, stirring occasionally, until the chocolate has melted. Spread over the top of each éclair.

PROFITEROLES WITH COFFEE MASCARPONE AND DARK CHOCOLATE SAUCE

PREPARATION 40 MINUTES
COOKING 45 MINUTES
MAKES 16

125 g (4½ oz/1 cup) plain (all-purpose) flour
70 g (2½ oz) unsalted butter, cubed
4 eggs, at room temperature

FILLING
2 tablespoons instant coffee granules
450 g (1 lb/2 cups) mascarpone cheese
2 tablespoons icing (confectioners') sugar

DARK CHOCOLATE SAUCE
100 g (3½ oz/⅔ cup) chopped dark chocolate
30 g (1 oz) unsalted butter
80 ml (2½ fl oz/1⅓ cups) cream

METHOD
Preheat the oven to 200°C (400°F/Gas 6). Lightly grease two baking trays. Sift the flour onto a piece of baking paper.

Put the butter, $\frac{1}{2}$ teaspoon salt and 250 ml (9 fl oz/ 1 cup) water in a saucepan and bring to the boil. Stir occasionally. Use the baking paper as a funnel to quickly pour the flour into the boiling mixture. Reduce heat to low, then beat vigorously until the mixture leaves the side of the pan and forms a smooth ball. Transfer to a bowl and set aside to cool. Using electric beaters, beat in the eggs, one at a time, until the mixture is thick and glossy.

Using two spoons, gently drop 16 rounded balls of the mixture about 3 cm ($1\frac{1}{4}$ inches) in diameter and 3 cm ($1\frac{1}{4}$ inches) apart onto the baking trays. Bake for 20 minutes, or until the balls are puffed. Reduce heat to 180°C (350°F/Gas 4) and bake for 10 minutes, or until the puffs are golden brown and crisp.

Using a small, sharp knife, gently slit the puffs to allow steam to escape. Return to the oven for 10 minutes, or until the insides are dry. Cool to room temperature.

To make the filling, dissolve the coffee in 1 tablespoon boiling water. Set aside to cool. Combine the coffee, mascarpone and icing sugar. Be careful not to overmix, or the mixture will separate.

To make the dark chocolate sauce, put the chocolate, butter and cream in a small heatproof bowl set over a pan of simmering water. Mix well then set aside to cool slightly. Just before serving, cut the profiteroles in half and sandwich together with the filling. Drizzle with the chocolate sauce.

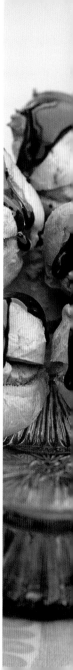

BAKED CHOCOLATE CHEESECAKE

PREPARATION 20 MINUTES
COOKING 1 HOUR 40 MINUTES
SERVES 8–10

125 g (4½ oz) plain chocolate biscuits (cookies)
40 g (1½ oz/¼ cup) chopped almonds
90 g (3¼ oz) unsalted butter, melted
1 tablespoon soft brown sugar

FILLING
500 g (1 lb 2 oz/2 cups) cream cheese, at room temperature
95 g (3¼ oz/½ cup) soft brown sugar
110 g (3¾ oz/¾ cup) chopped dark chocolate
125 ml (4 fl oz/½ cup) thick (double/heavy) cream
2 eggs, at room temperature, beaten
1 teaspoon grated orange zest
whipped cream, raspberries and chocolate
curls, to serve

METHOD

Brush a 20 cm (8 inch) spring-form cake tin with melted butter or oil and line the base with baking paper. Put the biscuits in a food processor with the almonds and process into crumbs.

Add the butter and sugar and process until they are combined. Press the mixture firmly into the base of the tin and refrigerate until firm. Preheat the oven to 160°C (315°F/Gas 2–3).

Put the chocolate in a heatproof bowl. Half fill a saucepan with water, bring to the boil, then remove from the heat and sit the bowl over the pan (don't let the bowl touch the water or the chocolate will get too hot and seize). Stir occasionally until the chocolate melts. Allow to cool.

To make the filling, beat the cream cheese and sugar until creamy. Blend in the cooled melted chocolate, cream, eggs and orange zest. Mix until smooth.

Pour the filling over the crumb crust and smooth the surface. Bake for 1 hour 20 minutes, or until the filling is firm to the touch.

Leave the cheesecake to cool in the tin and then refrigerate overnight. Top with whipped cream, fresh raspberries and chocolate curls.

RASPBERRY MERINGUE WHITE CHOCOLATE ROLL

PREPARATION 35 MINUTES
COOKING 15 MINUTES
SERVES 6–8

4 egg whites, at room temperature
170 g (6 oz/¾ cup) caster (superfine) sugar
125 g (4½ oz) cream cheese, softened
125 g (4½ oz/¾ cup) white chocolate
185 g (6 oz/¾ cup) sour cream
125 g (4½ oz/1 cup) raspberries

METHOD
Preheat the oven to 180°C (350°F/Gas 4). Line the base
and long sides of a 25 x 30 cm (10 x 12 inch) roasting
tin with baking paper.

Beat the egg whites until soft peaks form.
Gradually add the sugar, beating constantly. Beat
until the meringue is thick and glossy and the sugar
has dissolved.

Spread the mixture into the tin and bake for
10 minutes, or until lightly browned and firm to touch.
Quickly and carefully turn onto baking paper that has
been sprinkled with caster sugar. Leave to cool.

Put the white chocolate in a heatproof bowl. Half fill
a saucepan with water, bring to the boil, then remove
from the heat and sit the bowl over the pan (don't let
the bowl touch the water or the chocolate will get
too hot and seize). Stir occasionally until the chocolate
melts. Allow to cool.

Beat the cream cheese and sour cream until smooth
and creamy. Add the cooled white chocolate and beat
until smooth. Spread over the meringue base, leaving a
1 cm (½ inch) border. Top with a layer of raspberries.

Carefully roll the meringue, using the paper as a guide,
from one short end. Wrap firmly in the sugared
paper and plastic wrap and chill until firm. Cut into
slices and serve.

CHOCOLATE MALAKOFF

PREPARATION 30 MINUTES
COOKING 5 MINUTES
SERVES 6–8

100 ml (3½ fl oz) coffee liqueur
250 g (9 oz) small savoiardi (sponge finger biscuits)
50 g (1¾ oz/⅓ cup) chopped dark chocolate
125 g (4½ oz) unsalted butter, softened
145 g (6½ oz/⅔ cup) caster (superfine) sugar
½ teaspoon vanilla extract
125 g (4½ oz/1¼ cups) ground almonds
150 ml (5 fl oz) cream, whipped
150 g (5½ oz/1¼ cups) raspberries
unsweetened cocoa powder and icing
(confectioners') sugar, to dust
extra raspberries, to serve

METHOD
Line a 1.5 litre (52 fl oz/6 cup) pudding basin
(mould) with plastic wrap, allowing enough overhang
to use as handles when unmoulding. Mix half the
liqueur with 1 tablespoon water. Dip the smooth sides
of the savoiardi briefly into the liquid and use them to
neatly line the bottom and sides of the basin, placing
the smooth sides of the biscuits inwards.
Stand the biscuits upright around the side, and trim
them to fit snugly.

To melt the chocolate, put the chocolate in a heatproof bowl. Half fill a saucepan with water, bring to the boil, then remove from the heat and sit the bowl over the pan (don't let the bowl touch the water or the chocolate will get too hot and seize). Stir frequently. Remove the bowl from the pan and stir in the remaining coffee liqueur, including any liquid left over from dipping the biscuits.

Cream the butter and sugar with electric beaters until pale and fluffy. Fold in the melted chocolate. Add the vanilla and ground almonds and fold in lightly but thoroughly. Fold in the whipped cream.

Spoon one-quarter of the mixture into the basin. Cover with one-third of the raspberries, then continue layering and finish with the remaining one-quarter of the mixture smoothed over the top. If you have any biscuits left, they can go on top. Cover and refrigerate overnight to set.

Use the plastic wrap to lever the pudding out of the basin (you can also run a knife around the inside of the basin to help loosen it), then invert it onto a serving plate. Remove the plastic wrap. Dust the top with cocoa, letting some of it drift down the side. Lightly dust icing sugar on top of the cocoa. Cut into slices and serve with extra raspberries.

CHOCOLATE SWIRL PAVLOVA WITH DIPPED STRAWBERRIES

PREPARATION 30 MINUTES
COOKING 55 MINUTES
SERVES 8–10

60 g (2¼ oz/heaped ¾ cup) chopped dark chocolate
300 g (10½ oz) small to medium strawberries
4 egg whites, at room temperature
pinch of cream of tartar
230 g (8 oz/1 cup) caster (superfine) sugar
250 ml (9 fl oz/1 cup) cream, for whipping
1 tablespoon strawberry or raspberry liqueur
1 tablespoon icing (confectioners') sugar
3 tablespoons strawberry jam
1 tablespoon strawberry or raspberry liqueur, extra

METHOD

Melt the chocolate in a heatproof bowl over a
saucepan of simmering water. Don't let the base of
the bowl touch the water or the chocolate will get too
hot and seize. Dip eight of the strawberries partially
into the chocolate, then put them on a sheet of
baking paper and leave to set. Reserve the remaining
chocolate. Hull the rest of the strawberries, then cut
some in half lengthways, leaving the rest whole.
Refrigerate until needed.

Preheat the oven to 150°C (300°F/Gas 2). Grease a baking tray and line with baking paper. Using electric beaters, whisk the egg whites until firm peaks form. Add the cream of tartar, then the sugar in a slow, steady stream, beating continuously. Continue to beat for about 5 minutes until the meringue is glossy and very thick.

Spoon one-third of the meringue onto the tray and spread it into a rough 23 cm (9 inch) round. With a spoon, drizzle over one-third of the melted chocolate, making swirls of chocolate in a marbled effect. Top with more meringue and chocolate drizzle, then repeat once more. Use a metal spatula to flatten slightly and smooth the surface.

Bake for 50 minutes, or until the edges and top of the meringue are dry. Turn the oven off, leave the door ajar and allow the meringue to cool fully.

Beat the cream, liqueur and icing sugar until thick. Turn out onto a wire rack, peel off the baking paper and invert the pavlova onto a serving platter. Spread with whipped cream. Arrange whole and halved strawberries over the cream, interspersing them with chocolate-coated strawberries.

Warm the strawberry jam, then pass it through a sieve and stir in the liqueur. Use a pastry brush to coat the strawberries with the extra jam mixture, until they look glossy. Slice pavlova into thick wedges and serve.

CHOCOLATE AND CHESTNUT MARQUIS LOAF

PREPARATION 30 MINUTES
COOKING 5 MINUTES
SERVES 10–12

125 g (4½ oz/heaped ¾ cup) chopped dark chocolate
110 g (3¾ oz) tinned sweetened chestnut purée
1 tablespoon brandy
50 g (1¾ oz) unsalted butter, softened
2 tablespoons unsweetened cocoa powder
3 tablespoons caster (superfine) sugar
2 egg yolks, at room temperature
1 teaspoon powdered gelatine
170 ml (5½ fl oz/⅔ cup) cream, for whipping
raspberries, to serve
icing (confectioners') sugar, to dust

METHOD
Line a 6 x 17 cm (2½ x 6½ inch) loaf (bar) tin with
plastic wrap. Leave some overhang to assist with
turning out. Melt the chocolate in a small heatproof
bowl over a saucepan of simmering water. Don't let
the base of the bowl touch the water or the chocolate
will get too hot and seize. Stir frequently. Remove
from the heat and stir in the chestnut purée and
brandy. Allow to cool.

Using electric beaters, beat the butter, cocoa and half the sugar until creamy. In a separate small bowl, using electric beaters, beat the egg yolks and remaining sugar until creamy.

Put the gelatine in a small bowl with 2 teaspoons water. Set over a basin of hot water to dissolve the gelatine. In another bowl, beat the cream until firm peaks form, then set aside.

Using electric beaters, beat the cooled chocolate and chestnut mixture into the butter and cocoa mixture until smooth. Fold in the egg and gelatine, then fold in the beaten cream. Pour into the tin. Cover with the overlapping plastic and refrigerate for several hours, or overnight.

To serve, remove the marquis from the tin with the aid of the plastic wrap. Cut into thick slices while cold and place on serving plates. Dust the raspberries with icing sugar and serve to the side.

CHOCOLATE TUILES

PREPARATION 15 MINUTES
COOKING 35 MINUTES
MAKES 12

1 egg white, at room temperature
60 g (2¼ oz/¼ cup) caster (superfine) sugar
2 tablespoons plain (all-purpose) flour
30 g (1 oz) butter, melted
1 teaspoon vanilla extract
60 g (2 oz) dark chocolate melts, melted

METHOD
Preheat the oven to 180°C (350°F/Gas 4). Line two
baking trays with baking paper. Draw two 10 cm
(4 inch) circles on each sheet of paper.

Combine the egg white, sugar, flour, butter and vanilla
until a paste forms. Place the chocolate in a paper
piping (icing) bag, seal the end and snip off the tip.
Drizzle the chocolate over the baking paper in swirls,
following the marked circles. Allow the chocolate to set.

Spread 1½ teaspoons of the egg mixture over the
circles. Bake the tuiles, one tray at a time, for
4–6 minutes, or until the edges are just turning golden.
Remove from the oven and quickly shape each circle
over a rolling pin. Repeat until you have finished with
all of the mixture. Cool the tuiles until crisp.

HOT MOCHA SOUFFLE

PREPARATION 25 MINUTES
COOKING 45 MINUTES
SERVES 6-8

3 tablespoons caster (superfine) sugar
40 g (1½ oz) unsalted butter
2 tablespoons plain (all-purpose) flour
185 ml (6 fl oz/¾ cup) milk
1 tablespoon instant espresso-style coffee powder
100 g (3½ oz/⅔ cup) dark chocolate, melted
4 eggs, at room temperature, separated
icing (confectioners') sugar, to dust

METHOD

Preheat the oven to 180°C (350°F/Gas 4).
Wrap a double thickness of baking paper around a
1.25 litre (44 fl oz/5 cup) soufflé dish extending 3 cm
(1¼ inches) above the rim. Tie securely with string.
Brush with oil or melted butter, sprinkle 1 tablespoon
of the sugar into the dish, shake the dish to coat the
base and side evenly, then shake out any excess.

Melt the butter in a saucepan, add the flour and stir over low heat for 2 minutes, or until lightly golden. Gradually add the milk and stir until smooth. Stir over medium heat until the mixture boils and thickens, then boil for another minute. Remove from the heat and transfer to a large bowl.

Put the chocolate in a heatproof bowl. Half fill a saucepan with water, bring to the boil, then remove from the heat and sit the bowl over the pan (don't let the bowl touch the water or the chocolate will get too hot and seize). Stir occasionally until the chocolate melts and is smooth.

Dissolve the coffee in 1 tablespoon hot water, add to the milk mixture along with the remaining sugar, melted chocolate and egg yolks, then beat until smooth.

Beat the egg whites until stiff peaks form and then fold a little into the chocolate mixture to loosen it slightly. Gently fold in the remaining egg white, then spoon the mixture into the soufflé dish and bake for 40 minutes, or until well risen and just firm. Remove the collar, dust the soufflé with icing sugar and serve immediately.

CHOCOLATE MERINGUE KISSES

PREPARATION 20 MINUTES
COOKING 40 MINUTES
MAKES 25

2 egg whites, at room temperature
115 g (4 oz/½ cup) caster (superfine) sugar
¼ teaspoon ground cinnamon

FILLING
125 g (4½ oz) dark chocolate melts
90 g (3¼ oz/⅓ cup) sour cream

METHOD
Preheat the oven to 150°C (300°F/Gas 2). Line two
baking trays with baking paper.

Using electric beaters, beat the egg whites until
soft peaks form. Gradually add the sugar, beating
well after each addition. Beat until the sugar has
dissolved and the mixture is thick and glossy.
Add the cinnamon and beat well.

Transfer to a piping (icing) bag fitted with a 1 cm (½ inch) fluted nozzle. Pipe small stars of 1.5 cm (⅝ inch) diameter onto the trays 3 cm (1¼ inches) apart. Bake for 30 minutes, or until pale and crisp. Turn the oven off and cool with the door ajar.

To make the filling, place the chocolate and sour cream in a small heatproof bowl. Stand the bowl over a saucepan of simmering water. Stir until the chocolate has melted and the mixture is smooth. Remove from the heat and cool slightly.

Sandwich the meringues together with the filling and serve.

CHOCOLATE COFFEE MOUSSE MERINGUE CAKE

PREPARATION 20 MINUTES
COOKING 50 MINUTES
SERVES 10–12

6 eggs, at room temperature, separated
375 g (13 oz/1⅔ cups) caster (superfine) sugar
2½ tablespoons unsweetened cocoa powder,
plus extra to dust
1 tablespoon instant coffee granules
200 g (7 oz) dark chocolate
600 ml (21 fl oz) cream, whipped

METHOD
Preheat the oven to 150°C (300°F/Gas 2). Cut four
pieces of baking paper large enough to line four baking
trays. On three of the pieces of paper, mark a 22 cm
(8½ inch) circle. On the remaining piece, draw straight
lines, 3 cm (1¼ inches) apart. Line the baking trays
with the paper.

Beat the egg whites until soft peaks form. Gradually
add the sugar, beating well after each addition. Beat
for 5–10 minutes, until thick and glossy and all the
sugar has dissolved. Gently fold the sifted cocoa
into the meringue.

Divide the meringue into four portions. Spread three portions over each of the marked circles. Put the remaining meringue in a piping (icing) bag fitted with a 1 cm (½ inch) plain piping nozzle. Pipe lines about 8 cm (3¼ inches) long over the marked lines. Bake for 45 minutes, or until pale and crisp. Check the meringue strips occasionally to prevent overcooking. Turn the oven off and cool with the door ajar.

Put the chocolate in a heatproof bowl. Half fill a saucepan with water, bring to the boil, then remove from the heat and sit the bowl over the pan (don't let the bowl touch the water or the chocolate will get too hot and seize). Stir occasionally until the chocolate melts.

Dissolve the coffee granules in 1 tablespoon water. Put the melted chocolate in a bowl, whisk in the egg yolks and the coffee mixture, and beat until smooth. Fold in the whipped cream and mix well. Refrigerate until the mousse is cold and thick.

To assemble, place one meringue disc on a plate and spread with one-third of the mousse. Top with another disc and spread with half the remaining mousse. Repeat with the remaining disc and mousse. Run a knife around the edge of the meringue cake to spread the mousse evenly over the edge. Cut or break the meringue strips into short pieces and pile them on top of the cake, pressing them into the mousse. Dust with cocoa powder and refrigerate until firm.

CHOCOLATE LIQUEUR FRAPPE

PREPARATION 5 MINUTES
COOKING NIL
SERVES 2

260 g (9¼ oz/2 cups) ice cubes
125 ml (4 fl oz/½ cup) milk
60ml (2 fl oz/¼ cup) cream
2 tablespoons Frangelico
40 g (1½ oz/⅓ cup) icing (confectioners') sugar
2 tablespoons unsweetened cocoa powder,
plus extra, to dust

METHOD
Put the ice, milk, cream, Frangelico, icing sugar
and cocoa in a blender. Blend until thick and creamy.
Pour into tall glasses, dust with extra cocoa and serve.

COOKING WITH CHOCOLATE

People the world over know that eating a cake, cookie or pie made with chocolate promotes a feel-good sensation virtually unrivalled by any other foodstuff. When cooking with chocolate, it's important to buy the best you can afford because, while a rich flavour and smooth texture may come at a price, they're worth it. Chocolate is made with different percentages of cocoa butter (which gives it its melting qualities and determines its quality) and is also available in milk and white varieties.

•

WHAT TO LOOK FOR

Buy the type of chocolate stipulated in the recipe. Using a different type will very likely produce a less pleasing result.

•

For the best flavour, buy good-quality chocolate with a high cocoa butter content (at least 50 per cent). The higher the cocoa butter content, the darker and more bitter the chocolate and the more intense the flavour of the item you are making.

WHAT TO LISTEN FOR

If, when you break a piece off a chocolate bar, it makes a satisfying, clean, sharp 'snap' sound, you know you've got good-quality chocolate. Lower grades of chocolate make a dull, muffled breaking sound.

TYPES OF CHOCOLATE

Couverture A superior form of chocolate often used in the restaurant and patisserie trades. It needs to be tempered (heated and cooled) before use, a process that ensures the hardness and gloss of the finished product. Couverture melts and coats easily, has a glossy finish and an intense chocolate flavour. It is often sold in large blocks.

Dark, semi-sweet and bitter-sweet chocolate These have vanilla, sugar and cocoa butter added to them. Their sugar content and flavour vary, but they are all good for cooking. Good-quality dark chocolate is glossy, smooth and slightly reddish in colour. It snaps cleanly, melts easily and has a sweet, almost fruity smell.

Milk chocolate This has milk solids added to it and is much sweeter and creamier than dark chocolate. It is generally more useful as a coating or topping than as an ingredient in the baking process.

White chocolate Not a 'true' chocolate, white chocolate doesn't contain cocoa liquor. It usually contains milk powder, sugar and vanilla. Creamy-white and very sweet, it won't behave in the same ways as dark or milk chocolate when heated or cooked, so don't use it as a substitute for dark chocolate and only use it when it is specifically called for in a recipe.

Cooking chocolate Chocolate labelled as 'cooking chocolate' often contains vegetable fat instead of cocoa butter and doesn't have the same depth of flavour as dark chocolate. Chocolate chips and buttons are often made of this. Check the label on the packet before buying.

HOW TO STORE

Store chocolate in a cool place (approximately 18°C/64°F), but ideally not in the refrigerator. Avoid exposure to high humidity.

If the weather is very hot and you must store chocolate in the refrigerator, place it in an airtight container and bring it to room temperature before removing it from the container. This will prevent condensation forming on the surface of the chocolate. Water droplets will prevent the chocolate from melting smoothly and may affect the texture of the melted chocolate.

Frequent exposure to high temperatures can cause the cocoa butter in chocolate to rise to the surface, creating a dusty appearance or 'bloom'. This can be corrected by melting and tempering the chocolate. Bloom can also indicate that the chocolate is past its use-by date (an unlikely scenario in most chocolate lover's homes).

Chocolate is very sensitive to odours, so store in a non-porous container well away from strong-smelling foods.

INDEX

Published in 2009 by Murdoch Books Pty Limited

Chief Executive: Juliet Rogers
Publishing Director: Kay Scarlett

Commissioning Editor: Lynn Lewis
Senior Designer: Heather Menzies
Editor: Kim Rowney
Project Editor: Kate Fitzgerald
Production: Elizabeth Malcolm
Photographers: Jared Fowler (internals);
Brett Stevens (cover)
Stylist: Cherise Koch
Recipes: Murdoch Books test kitchen

Murdoch Books Australia
Pier 8/9, 23 Hickson Road
Millers Point NSW 2000
Phone: +61 (0) 2 8220 2000
Fax: +61 (0) 2 8220 2558
www.murdochbooks.com.au

Murdoch Books UK Limited
Erico House, 6th Floor
93–99 Upper Richmond Road
Putney, London SW15 2TG
Phone: +44 (0) 20 8785 5995
Fax: +44 (0) 20 8785 5985
www.murdochbooks.co.uk

NOTE: For fan-forced ovens, set the oven temperature to 20°C (35°F) lower than indicated in the recipe. We have used 20 ml tablespoon measures. Seasonal availabilities are given only as a guide; regional differences may apply.

National Library of Australia Cataloguing-in-Publication
Title: My Little Chocolate Book
ISBN: 9781741966213 (pbk.)
Notes: Includes index.
Subjects: Cookery (Chocolate)
Chocolate.
Other Authors/Contributors: Lewis, Lynn.
Dewey Number: 641.6374
A catalogue record for this book is available from the British Library.

PRINTED IN CHINA